Robin Bush needs no introduction to anyone who knows Somerset, and few people could be better qualified to be the author of so delightful a book. He was educated at Exeter College, Oxford, lives in Taunton, and is Deputy County Archivist at Somerset Record Office, where, over the last twenty-five years, he has unearthed most of the stories now included here.

Many will have attended his lectures on various aspects of Somerset's past, and many more will have heard his regular weekly broadcasts on BBC Radio Bristol and BBC Somerset Sound. His involvement in the life of Somerset is immense. He is the author of many books on the county, including histories of Taunton, Wellington, Martock and Crewkerne. He has performed widely with the Taunton Operatic Society and the Somerset Opera Group, and is on the Council of Management of the Brewhouse Theatre. He is a former Chairman of the Somerset Archaeological and Natural History Society.

FRONTISPIECE
*The tower of St Michael's Church
on Glastonbury Tor, 1788.*

SOMERSET STORIES

Life & Laughter in Old Somerset

ROBIN BUSH

THE DOVECOTE PRESS

First published in 1990 by The Dovecote Press Ltd
Stanbridge, Wimborne, Dorset BH21 4JD

ISBN 0 946159 84 X

Photoset in Palatino by The Typesetting Bureau Ltd
Wimborne, Dorset
Printed and bound by Biddles Ltd,
Guildford and King's Lynn

CONTENTS

INTRODUCTION

I FIRST came to live in Somerset in 1967 after working for nearly two years in Surrey. I had been brought up in Devon and made occasional forays across the border with the Exeter School historical society, exploring the delights of predictable attractions such as Glastonbury, Wells and Bath, but I never got to know the county really well.

In the days when I arrived in Taunton I had no car and had never even taken a driving test. That was no handicap when it came to traversing the beautiful and nearby Quantock Hills on foot. I well remember one particular Bank Holiday Monday taking the train to Crowcombe Station, prior to the fall of the Beeching axe, walking up to Triscombe and along the ancient ridgeway to Crowcombe Park Gate, before dropping down into Crowcombe itself, soon to become one of my favourite villages. While walking around the superb parish church I met and subsequently befriended the then rector, the late Preb. Patrick Cowley. I recall that we shared an interest in the history of church houses in the county, not to mention a couple of pints in the Carew Arms. Soon after, I was invited to spend a weekend at Crowcombe as the guest of Preb. Cowley and his wife. That first morning, when I woke in the corner bedroom of the Tudor rectory and looked through the early mists across the valley towards the Brendon Hills, I decided that this could well be the county in which I would lay my bones.

I came to Somerset as an archivist at Somerset Record Office and am still, for my sins, an archivist. I and my colleagues labour unceasingly (which is my story !) at the Record Office where we collect, conserve and make available for study this county's written heritage. In the course of my work I have inevitably encountered an almost endless succession of Somerset characters: the sad, the successful, the humourous, the eccentric and the downright ridiculous. The result is that I tend to have even more friends and acquaintances in past centuries than in the present. Many of these I owe to our searchers: members of the general public and visitors from overseas who have come to us to trace their families, the history of their houses or to reconstruct the way in which particular villages or towns have developed or, occasionally, died.

Some six years ago, at the suggestion of my friend, Clinton Rogers, I began each week to share my stories with a wider audience, firstly on BBC Radio Bristol and more recently on BBC Somerset Sound. Among those who have regularly welcomed me onto their programmes have been the aforesaid Mr Rogers, Sheelagh Leigh-Ewers, Al Read, Simon White, Lisa Browne, Steve Haigh and Richard Austin. Some 300 broadcasts later, I have decided to make a more permanent record of a number of these contributions. Having to come up with a new topic every week, while continuing to pursue my full-time labours as Deputy County Archivist, has given me an increased respect for veterans such as Alaister Cooke, and I do not deceive myself that I have always succeeded.

I make no apology for casting doubts on some long-cherished beliefs which have bedevilled Somerset's guide-books. An awful lot of nonsense is still regularly retailed about such subjects as the Monmouth Rebellion and the early history of Glastonbury Abbey, let alone the links between Mells and Little Jack Horner.

Many of these tales have also been aired on innumerable occasions in talks delivered throughout the county and beyond, under such titles as 'Life and Laughter in Old Somerset' and 'Somerset as Was'. Very few of those which I have included in this volume have been published before and I have tried in each case to add something new to the study of Somerset's past from my own researches. I have not felt it necessary to confine myself to the truncated Somerset of post-1974, but in several chapters have strayed across that ill-conceived boundary which sadly separates us from our former brethren in Avon. Here, then, is a selection from my files – a relatively unsubtle blend of comment, humour, narrative and the occasional discovery.

I must acknowledge several ideas or suggestions from my present and former colleagues at the Somerset Record Office: Derek Shorrocks, Susan Berry, Steven Hobbs and Celia Parker. My friend, David Bromwich, at Somerset's Local History Library, has assisted me over the years with his unrivalled knowledge of printed sources relating to the county.

ROBIN BUSH

1

THE RECTOR VANISHES

A T 5.30 pm on 8 January 1868 the Rev Benjamin Speke, for nearly eleven years rector of Dowlish Wake, near Ilminster, walked out of a hatter's shop in Pimlico – and disappeared.

The Speke family have been settled in the West Country from the earliest times. Their earliest traceable member was the mid-12th century Richard Espec, believed to have been Steward of the Household to Robert FitzRegis, illegitimate son of King Henry I. He gained by marriage the manor of Brampford in Devon which, as a result, is known as Brampford Speke to this day. The surname itself seems to derive from an English nickname for the woodpecker. Richard's descendant in the eighth generation, Sir John Speke (died 1442), was a noted naval commander and MP. By his marriage to Joan Keynes the Spekes inherited the manor of Dowlish Wake, near Ilminster, a match which was to bring the family to Somerset. In fact the blood of the Wakes has since flowed in Speke veins for Joan was herself ninth in descent from Ralph Wake, lord of Dowlish manor in the 12th century: a lordship that has never been sold since that time and is today held still by Peter Speke of Rowlands, near Ilminster.

The senior branch of the Speke family acquired White Lackington, to the east of Ilminster, served as MPs and sheriffs of Somerset and backed the Royalist side during the Civil War. One of their number, Charles Speke, was executed after the Monmouth Rebellion of 1685, supposedly for indicating support for the luckless duke by shaking his hand. In reality it was Charles's older brother John who had been the active supporter, but he had fled and Judge Jeffreys reportedly asserted that the Speke family 'owe us a life'. This elder branch died out in an heiress who carried the family estates, including Dillington House, to her husband, the Prime Minister, Frederick Lord North, later Earl of Guilford.

A junior branch settled at Jordans (a house demolished in 1964) in Ashill, although retaining both the manor and the living of Dowlish Wake, the latter served as rector by two younger sons during the 18th century. A third, Hugh Speke, rector 1827-56, evidently considering the existing parsonage unsuitable, being described in 1815 as 'a poor, mean house', built Wake Hill House in the north of the parish. Thus it was into Wake Hill House that Hugh's nephew, the Rev Benjamin Speke, moved on his institution in 1857 as rector of Dowlish Wake.

The mission which took the Rev Benjamin to London on 8 January 1868 was to officiate at a friend's wedding. He travelled up by train from Ilminster and was expected at the Eccleston Square house of his brother-in-law, Charles Murdoch, MP for Reading. After his depositing his luggage at the house and without making his arrival known to the family, he abruptly left. It was later discovered that he had bought a hat in Warwick Street, Pimlico, but with his exit from the hatter's shop all trace of him was lost.

The family was naturally distraught. Benjamin was the fourth son of his parents. The eldest son, William, had been married since 1850 but had produced no children. The second son had been the famous explorer, Capt John Hanning Speke, discoverer of the source of the Nile and a national hero until his death, unmarried, in a tragic shooting accident four years before. To his funeral at Dowlish Wake had come the rich and famous, including the intrepid Dr David, 'I presume', Livingstone. The third son, Edward, had been killed before Delhi in the Indian Mutiny of 1857, also unmarried. Benjamin, still a bachelor in 1868, was the remaining hope of his family.

The services of the Metropolitan detectives were called in but, when no trace of the missing cleric could be found, a reward of £100 was offered and advertisements were inserted in all the London papers. Benjamin, aged 37, was described as 5ft 9ins tall, with broad shoulders, grey eyes, dark hair and whiskers but with no beard or moustache, and 'a little bald on the top of his head'. He had been dressed in dark clothes and a dark overcoat, striped grey necktie, high hat with mourning band, silver watch with the initials B.S. on all his linen and was believed to have about £20 on his person. All that was elicited by these efforts was the discovery of his original hat in Birdcage Walk, whereupon the family in desperation increased the reward to the very considerable sum of £500 and Benjamin's brother William travelled to London to help in the search.

As can be imagined, the national press fell on the story with barely-concealed glee. It was supposed that the rector had been decoyed into a cab in Birdcage Walk and murdered for his money, his hat falling off during the attack. Rumours spread of a hastily-excavated grave in Birdcage Walk, of a body discovered in a Pimlico house and another in an Essex stream. He was supposed to have been traced to a lunatic asylum in Germany or to have embarked on a mission to Ethiopia to persuade King Theodore to abandon some of his 'spiritual wives'. The *Pall Mall Gazette*, however, claimed that Speke had similarly disappeared on a previous occasion some six to eight years before, on breaking off an intended marriage, and had later turned up in Paris.

Two weeks passed with no further news: but then in late February the scene transferred to Cornwall. Sergt Soady of Padstow had been issued with details of an absconded bankrupt and, seeing a man sitting on a gate, dressed as a bullock drover, who he considered fitted the description, took him into custody. After persistent questioning and the discovery of £200 in notes and gold on his person, the unfortunate man admitted that he was none other than the missing rector. He described how he had travelled to Basingstoke the first night, walked to Winchester the next day and then worked his way west to Cornwall.

According to the published accounts, Speke declared that he had become convinced that his family were indifferent to him. He had intended to lie low until the furore over his disappearance had died down and then take ship for America. There he had hoped to work for his living and preach the gospel to his fellow labourers. The true cause was his family's opposition to a marriage with his first cousin, with whom he had fallen deeply in love. He was dispatched to France to recuperate, but not before the Press had witnessed him enjoying a performance of *School for Scandal* from a box at Drury Lane Theatre.

One rather unhappy sequel was the question of the £500 reward. This the family handed over in full to Col Gilbert, Chief Constable of Cornwall. Gilbert, however, divided the money between his Deputy Chief Constable and his Superintendent, causing an outcry in the papers that Sergt Soady, the actual solver of the mystery, had received nothing. A lighter footnote is provided by a poem which appeared in the *Judy*, a contemporary magazine rival to *Punch*, although the verse was hardly Tennysonian in its quality!

> *The Reverend B. Speke*
> *Cut away from his sheep,*
> *They couldn't tell where to find him:*
> *When he started alone*
> *On his travels to roam,*
> *He left his old hat behind him.*
>
> *To his flock and his church*

Which he'd left in the lurch
That he didn't come back they wondered.
They pasted the boards
with bills of rewards
Till they made it a round 'five hundred'.

About missing Speke
Of letters a heap
His friends in the papers publish,
Each spoke his suggestion
About the Speke question,
But it all in the end proved rubbish.

They dug in the park
And they groped in the dark
And made such a bother about him,
Till detectives looked wise
And began to surmise
They'd have to come home without him.

The store shops 'marine'
And the sausage machines
They searched for a bone or a button,
But the cupboard was bare
And not even a hair
Could they find, so reward they gone none!

And so on it went,
Till surmised were spent,
And they looked in unSPEKEable places,
Whilst all the time snug,
Like a flea in a rug,
Mr Speke at his seekers made faces.

When a mint it had cost,
And all gave up for lost,
Burked or kidnapped, the clerical rover,
At Padstow one day
They arrested the gay
Mr Speke in disguise of a drover!

In due course the Rev Benjamin Speke returned to Dowlish Wake and just over a year later, in May 1869, he married his first cousin, Caroline

Fuller, evidently the lady of whom his family had disapproved. Both their mothers were daughters of William Hanning of Dillington House. Clearly a love match, the couple had no fewer than seven sons and one daughter although sadly they were to enjoy less than twelve years together.

Benjamin's beloved passed away at noon on 23 February 1881 from 'congestion of the lungs' after a long illness. Worn out with sharing her struggle for life and frantic with grief, Benjamin evidently decided that he could not live without her and the very next morning he drowned himself in a deep tank in the shrubbery at Wake Hill House. The couple were buried together in Dowlish Wake churchyard five days later. The village schoolchildren walked in procession behind the coffins while nearly a thousand people lined the lane down from Wake Hill House to the church. So ended one of the most poignant love stories in the history of Somerset.

BURIALS in the Parish of _Dowlish Wake_ in the County of _Somerset_ in the Year 18_81_				
Name.	Abode.	When buried.	Age.	By whom the Ceremony was performed.
Caroline Sophia Speke No. 513.	Wakehill	March 1	41	G. J. Gowring Offg Minr
Benjamin Speke No. 514.	Rector of Dowlish Wakehill	March 1	50	G. J. Gowring Offg Minr

Burial entries for Caroline Sophia and her husband, the Rev Benjamin Speke, from Dowlish Wake parish register: 1 March 1881.

2

THE VIKING PUB

JUST south of Weston-super-Mare on the A370 at Lympsham stands the Hobbs Boat Inn. In December 1985 the inn reopened after an extensive programme of redecoration which included the joys of an 'olde worlde' 50-seat steak bar. Publicity releases at the time recalled the story as to how the inn got its unusual name.

According to the *Weston Mercury* the inn sign derived from 'the funeral of the Viking King Hubba who in traditional Viking style was buried in his boat, which was set on fire and pushed down the River Axe. On the turn of the tide the boat came back up the river and settled near to the site of the pub. The Vikings were plundering nearby when an old lady named Hobbs cut the ropes of their boats, which drifted out to sea, leaving the marauding Vikings unprotected.'

The origin of this story, unlike so many allegedly handed down from generation to generation in rural areas of England, can be precisely dated to only just over a century ago. No-one had ever considered the possibility that Hubba, or Ubbi as he is usually called in contemporary chronicles, raided the Somerset coast in the area of Weston-super-Mare until 1875. In that year the Roman Catholic bishop of Clifton, William Clifford, published a paper in the *Proceedings of the Somerset Archaeological Society* in which he argued from place-name evidence that the mouth of the Axe was the site of Hubba's raid.

The Anglo-Saxon Chronicle dates the raid to 878 but does not mention Hubba by name, stating only that 'the same winter the brother of Ivar and Healfdene was in the kingdom of the West Saxons with 23 ships. And he was killed there and 80 men of his army with him. And there was captured the banner which they called 'Raven'.' The identification of their leader with Ubbi, the son of Ragnar Lothbrok, was considered far from certain by Sir Frank Stenton. Ragnar was the most famous Viking of the ninth century and, according to one Scandinavian story, died when Osberht threw him into a pit of snakes. Bishop Asser, in his contemporary life of King Alfred, claimed that the Viking raiders came from South Wales and describes the siege of a fort called Cynwit.

Hubba the Dane glowers from the inn sign at Lympsham.

Somerset historians formerly identified this Cynwit with Cannington, shifted the site of the raid to Bridgwater Bay and even tentatively claimed a burial mound now within the confines of Hinckley Point Nuclear Power Station as the final resting place of Hubba the Dane. The early forms of the name Cannington, however, do not square with a corrupted form of Cynwit and show that Cannington developed from 'Cantuctun', recorded c.880 and meaning the tun or settlement by the Quantock Hills. Two versions of the account of the raid in the Anglo-Saxon Chronicle add that it took place in Devon and place-name scholars have shown that Cynwit was Countisbury in North Devon, deriving from the British 'Cunet'. Hubba or Ubbi was therefore unknown to Somerset even if he could be correctly identified as the leader of the raid of 878.

If neither Hubba nor the redoubtable Saxon lady called Hobbs supplied the inn with its name, how did it originate ? Rate books, alehouse licences and Land Tax assessments for Lympsham enable the inn to be traced back to at least 1761 when it was operated by Robert Hardwidge. An initial clue is given in John Rutter's *New Guide to Weston-super-Mare* of 1840 which refers to 'an elevated causeway passing by the little inn, whose sign, Hobb's Boat, records the ancient ferry over the Axe'. Collinson, the county historian, writing in 1791, mentions 'the river Ax, over which, one mile north from the church, is a ferry-boat for horses when the tide is in; but at ebb tide the river is not more than two feet deep. This ferry has the name of Hobb's boat.'

Before the Reformation the manor of Lympsham was one of the many possessions of Glastonbury Abbey. Among the free tenants as early as 1234 was William Harold who paid 8d a year for the passage or ferry with half an acre of land. I eventually discovered the origin of the inn's name, however, in a later survey of the abbey's lands commissioned by Abbot Richard Bere in 1515-16. There it is stated that the passage or ferry 'next Justyneshayes' was held for 5s. a year, with other lands, by one – Thomas Hobbs. The ferryman gave his name to his ferry and the ferry to an inn, a name which it still bears over four and a half centuries later.

My solution to the puzzle is prosaic compared with the legendary Viking whose image still adorns the inn sign at Lympsham but it happens to be the truth.

3

Unnatural Death

ON 6 October 1320 William le Faunt had been drinking in William Mere's tavern at Williton. That night, while travelling home to Carhampton through the hamlet of Stream, he got into an argument with Henry Beauflower. Their quarrel ended with Faunt striking Henry on the head with a door bar and killing him outright. Faunt thereupon took fright and fled. Ten days later an inquest was held by the coroner for West Somerset, attended by men from all the adjoining villages: Nettlecombe, Monksilver and Old Cleeve, as well as from Williton itself. In Faunt's absence, they seized and valued his pathetic collection of worldly goods – a pig at 2s, a sea fish trap at 4s, a net at 3s and a shelter (to protect himself on the sea shore while fishing ?) at 1s. Under the old custom of deodand the men of Williton also suffered, having to hand over the value of the door bar, one halfpenny, which had caused Henry's death.

The records kept by Somerset coroners have generally been poorly preserved, evidently because successive holders of that office seem to have regarded them as their personal property. Thus hardly any survive from before the present century with the exception of a few, mainly of the 18th century, for the boroughs of Langport and Bridgwater. Fortunately, Douglas Stevens, a retired headmaster and local historian living at Minehead, discovered among the archives of the Luttrells of Dunster Castle a coroner's roll for the years 1315 to 1321 and later published it. A fascinating document, it details all the 58 inquests held by the coroner, Sir Ralph FitzUrse, great-great-great nephew of Sir Reginald FitzUrse, one of the knights who murdered Thomas a Becket.

Although a catalogue of six years of violent death may present an unduly harsh picture of medieval life, it still gives us an illuminating slant on everyday affairs over six and a half centuries ago. Six men literally starved to death. John le Comere from Bristol was found on the Quantocks dead from 'hunger and helplessness', William Horny collapsed while coming away from Wellington market, Roger Potel of Brompton Ralph passed out while begging at Chipstable and Robert le Vayre,

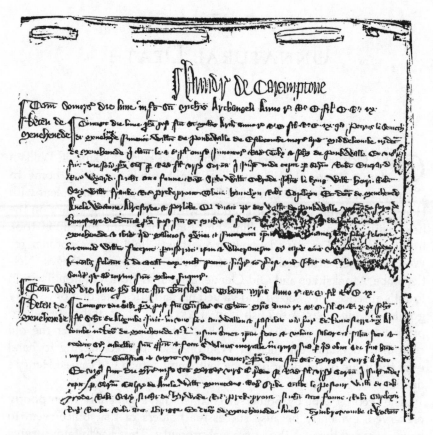

The first membrane of the Coroner's roll for West Somerset, 1315-20. The heading reads 'the Hundred of Caramptone' [Carhampton] and the first inquest was held on Monday the feast of St Michael the Archangel in the 9th year of King Edward son of Edward [Edward II]. The tithing in which each death took place is given in the left-hand margin, starting with Menehevede [Minehead].

having landed from Wales, 'lay down at Dunster harbour and died by misadventure of wretchedness and want'.

Four men suffering from the 'falling sickness', as epilepsy was known, died as a result of fits: one in an oxhouse at Fairfield in Stogursey and another in Sir Andrew Luttrell's stable at East Quantoxhead. Children were as much at risk as they are today. William le Taillour, only 16 weeks old, burned to death in his cot before his father's fire at Hawkwell, and Richard Nogher of Porlock found his two-year-old daughter Ellen drowned after she fell into a spring trying to reach an apple that she had dropped. At Periton in Minehead Gilbert le Tournour, aged 1½, up a knife from his father's bench and fell on it, while toddling towards the hall door, and at Exford John Broun, 2½, fell into a well and drowned. Indeed, drowning was the most common cause of unnatural death. Avice atte Halleheghen died in the sea at Grey Cliff in Old Cleeve while trying to load a fishing boat, and at Hagley in Milverton Robert le Toukere fell into the River Tone as he was trying to lop alder branches for firewood.

Two women were killed by the weather. Eghelina de Harwode was walking home to Stoke Pero from Molton in Devon on Christmas Eve 1320 but, while crossing Exmoor at Bellbrook, 'night and snow overcame her and buried her body, whereby she died by misadventure'. Her father Nicholas went out to search for her and discovered her body. That same month Denise of Kingsbrompton was returning from Withiel Mill on foot to beg when 'snow and weakness overcame her and weighed her down' on Hurscombe Hill. There were other tragedies caused by those who became unhinged. One night in 1321 at Bridgwater John de Burgoyne went beserk in his father Thomas's house and tried to kill his brothers and sisters. Thomas attempted to restrain him and was stabbed to death by his son. Gunnilda Foghyn of Old Cleeve went mad and cut the throat of three-year-old Cecily le Lange. The jury valued the knife at a halfpenny and the coroner ordered Gunnilda to the county gaol, then located at Somerton.

Others perished in a whole variety of ways: beams, branches, chimneys and walls fell on them: they slipped into wells and streams, fell from barn lofts and off bridges into streams. John Sone was driving his sheep from their fold to pasture at Wood in Williton when he was struck by a thunderbolt and 'died immediately by contrivance of the Devil'.

And of course there was murder. William de Poukewalle of East Luccombe was on his way home from Dunster market when he was attacked and killed at Minehead by unknown strangers. The three burglars who broke into the house of Richard le Elyman at Sandhill in Withycombe and slew him also escaped justice. One-eyed John of Congresbury, who had entered the house of Alice de Behull's house in Heathcombe at twilight, killed her, stole her goods and fled. In 1315 four unknown men had breakfast at Gilbert le Fisshere's house at Halse and agreed to go to Bampton fair. Between Preston Priors and Milverton, at a place called Gorrenhende, two of them fell on a third and cut his throat, knocking the fourth man unconscious because he refused to help them.

There was one occasion, however, in 1316, when the law did manage to identify the murderers. Ralph and Henry de Prestcote from Cutcombe, probably brothers, with the connivance of William of Withycombe,

The former market-place at Dunster. The Luttrell Arms stands on the left of the picture, the covered Yarn Market in the foreground and the castle of the Luttrells rises behind. The scene is little changed today apart from the proliferation of gift shops and yellow lines. William de Poukewalle was on his way home from Dunster market to East Luccombe when he was murdered at Minehead in 1315.

attacked Richard de Herdecombe at an isolated spot called Stetfold Rocks at Almsworthy in Winsford. They beat him about the head and shoulders, fatally wounding him. He lived long enough to receive the last rites of the church and, presumably, to identify his assailants. The Prestcotes' goods were seized, comprising four bullocks, two cows, one of them 'weak', three calves, four heifers, one mare, a pig, five wether sheep, and three ewes in lamb, valued in total at 42s. The bailiff of the hundred of Free Manors was required to arrest the Prestcotes and their accessory and convey all three to Somerton gaol.

The dangers of the motorcar and the juggernaut lorry may have been unknown, but the ways in which the 14th century people of Somerset might go to meet their Maker were still infinitely varied.

4
WHIGGISH CHRISTENINGS

IT was a quiet afternoon at the Somerset Record Office and, believe you me, there are precious few of those these days. One of our searchers came over to me bearing a 19th century parish register of Ilchester and pointed out that on 23 May 1818 23 infants were baptised there with the christian names Merest or Coffin or both. A further five such baptisms occurred on 19 June, including the exotically named James Isaac Merest Coffin Bolton Hallett. Quite naturally our searcher asked me what possible reason 28 totally unrelated sets of parents could have for taking such unanimous action. To be honest, I hadn't a clue.

After consulting several standard works on Somerset's history in general and Ilchester's in particular, with a consummate lack of success, I turned to the *Western Flying Post*, the newspaper that in those days circulated throughout the four south-western counties. There, finally, I found my answer.

Ilchester in the early 19th century was still the county town of Somerset and, although it had less than a thousand inhabitants, continued to return two Members of Parliament as it had done since 1298. Elections there had generally been dominated by the Phelips family of Montacute House in the 17th century, except when they were opposed by the Strodes of Barrington Court. Thereafter control passed to the Lockyer and other families, the price of a vote in bribes rising from two guineas in 1702 to £30 in 1784.

In 1802 Sir William Manners, a Tory borough monger, paid the phenomenal sum of £53,000 for the patronage of the borough and for much of the property there. After the 1812 election, evidently finding it too expensive to bribe the existing electorate, Manners took the incredible step of demolishing a hundred houses in the borough, leaving only some sixty standing. His homeless tenants, disqualified from voting, were then housed in a workhouse hired by Ilchester Corporation from Manners. At one point Manners even threatened to pull the workhouse down. The strength of feeling in Ilchester against him can only be imagined.

When Baptized.	Child's Christian Name.	Parents Name.		Abode.	Quality, Trade, or Profession.	By whom the Ceremony was performed.
		Christian.	Surname.			
1818 23. May No. 105.	William Merest Coffin son of	James Sarah	Gear	Ilchester	Laborer	T. Ebrey Rector
23. May No. 106.	Matilda Merest Coffin daughter	John Ann	Arnold	Ilchester	Vender of Medicines	T. Ebrey Rector
23. May No. 107.	Robert Merest Coffin son of	Robert Mary	Ivms	Ilchester	Mason	T. Ebrey Rector
23. May No. 108.	Elizabeth Merest Coffin daughter	Charles Martha	Chene	Ilchester	Mason	T. Ebrey Rector
23. May No. 109.	Harriet Merest Coffin daughter	Thomas Ann	Pope	Ilchester	Laborer	T. Ebrey Rector
23. May No. 110.	John Merest Coffin son of	Charles Elizabeth	Pitman	Ilchester	Carpenter	T. Ebrey Rector
23. May No. 111.	William Merest Coffin son of	William Rachel	West	Ilchester	Thather	T. Ebrey Rector
23. May No. 112.	George Merest Coffin son of	Amelia	Harvey	Seamstress Ilchester		T. Ebrey Rector

A page of eight Merest Coffin christenings from Ilchester parish register: 23 May 1818.

Ilchester Mead: Lord Darlington's Liberal answer to homeless voters and to a pressing political problem.

Some six years later there appeared on the scene Lord Darlington, a Whig borough monger, to take advantage of the illfeeling which Manners had generated in Ilchester. Darlington leased land outside the town from the Corporation for a substantial amount to alleviate their financial problems. There he built the two large tenement blocks, which still stand, called Ilchester Mead and filled them with those people that Manners had evicted.

Thus when the next election came round on 17 June 1818 the two Whig candidates were returned at the head of the poll, defeating the Tories, one of whom was Manners's son, by 64 votes to 24. The new MPs were John William Drage Merest from Norfolk and Admiral Sir Isaac Coffin, Baronet. Problem solved!

It would seem that the rector of Ilchester, Thomas Ebrey, was having a round-up of the unbaptised. Clearly disgusted by the Tories' electoral tactics, he managed to persuade 28 sets of parents, possibly including several of those whom Manners had turned onto the streets, to name their children after the Whig candidates: 23 of them over three weeks before the election and 5 of them two days after. It has to be one of the longest-lasting and strangest political demonstrations on record.

5
EUREKA

THE unexpected in the life of an archivist is what adds that extra dimension to a profession that is already a fascinating and a rewarding one. Often it is the historically insignificant items that are to me the most fascinating.

Periodically, some long-established firms of solicitors have relieved the pressure on their bulging strong-rooms by transferring non-current deeds and other documents to local record offices. Such records are often vital material for local history but, by their very nature, they are rarely very personal or human archives. Judge of my delight when, going through a sizeable collection deposited by the Crewkerne solicitors, Sparks and Blake, I found a folded card, trimmed with lace, addressed to Silvester Bean, Esq., Mrs Osborn's, Allen's Row, Widcombe, Bath. It was dated 14 February 1810 and bore the following handwritten verse.

> Come to my aid ye lovely sisters nine.
>> Instruct my pen, inspire each fervent line.
> Can I be blam'd if I so true aspire
>> To win a youth that I so much admire?
> Ambition is no crime – but when wrong bent,
>> Can it be wrong fix'd on what's excellent?
> Ah, no – my heart exults in its design
>> To win my Silvester for my Valentine.

The unexpected Valentine which turned up among the papers of a Crewkerne solicitor: sent to Silvester Bean at Bath in 1810.

[24]

It would be nice to think that the anonymous lady did indeed win her Silvester.

A couple of years ago I was called in by some friends of mine at Kingston St Mary to advise them on some family papers which had lain gathering dust in a box in their loft. It then transpired that my host was a collateral descendant of Admiral Lord Gambier (1756-1833), Commander-in-Chief of the Mediterranean fleet at the height of the Napoleonic Wars. Among the accumulated papers were his Mediterranean log book and, because Gambier was the chief negotiator at Ghent in 1814 to end the war with America, there were also the almost daily despatches from Downing Street, all signed by Lord Castlereagh, then Prime Minister. I seized gleefully on a note signed by the Iron Duke of Wellington and then found myself reading a lengthy letter written from the admiral's cabin of HMS *Victory*, dated only weeks before the Battle of Trafalgar. If you were a historian looking for one of the last and hitherto unknown letters that Lord Nelson ever wrote, would you consider searching through the loft of a house in the Quantock Hills?

On another occasion I was asked by a charming couple named Clatworthy to call at their Long Sutton cottage to collect some family farming records for deposit at the Record Office. The Clatworthys and their ancestors, the Blakes, had formerly farmed at Cutsey in the parish of Trull, a few miles to the south of Taunton. The family had some years before handed over to the Record Office a substantial collection of deeds and leases to us and the old trunk that I had come for had been overlooked at the time of the previous turn-out.

Mr and Mrs Clatworthy had pulled the trunk on to the hearth-rug in front of fireplace and I remember how we got down on our respective knees around it. The documents were a mixture of the personal and the legal: letters, deeds, leases and the like, mainly from the 18th and 19th centuries. Finally, when we were about to conclude and decant the records into the archive boxes which I had brought with me, I reached into the trunk and pulled out a folded paper volume covered in worn parchment. When I opened it, I found myself looking at the Trull churchwardens' accounts for the early years of the reign of Henry VIII - a volume whose existence was until then totally unknown.

Somerset has a climate which the writer and wit, the Rev Sydney Smith of Combe Florey, charitably described as 'moist'. Such weather is not kind to the survival of paper records and, had this Trull document remained in its parish chest for four and a half centuries, I have little doubt that it would have quietly mouldered away. An endorsement on the cover indicated that it had been produced as evidence in a court case in the early 17th century. The Blake churchwarden of that time had simply forgotten to replace it in the church after the case had ended. Generations of domestic heating had been kinder to the book than would have been the cold, possibly damp, environment of Trull parish church. Thanks to the inadvertent care of the Clatworthys and their ancestors, those accounts have now joined a mere handful of similar pre-Reformation churchwardens' accounts that survive in Somerset from such an early period.

There are undoubtedly many documentary treasures still to be discovered in the Somerset Record Office itself. A large proportion of deposits remain uncatalogued or only summarily listed because of the sheer bulk concerned. In the last twenty years the rapid growth of interest in genealogy, 'tracing your roots', has meant that archivists have had progressively less time to devote to listing the collections committed to their charge.

One recent discovery was made not by an archivist but by a visiting American researching the early history of drama. In going through one substantial deposit of records he came across a bundle of letters written from London by Henry Bluett, occasionally to his father, John, at Kittisford, near Wellington, but mainly to his uncle, Richard Weekes, at Wiveliscombe, between 1608 and 1616. Weekes was comparatively well-off and young Bluett was something of a spendthrift who executed minor commissions for his uncle in the metropolis. The letters, almost without exception, were devoted to asking for money. Bluett's clothes got lost or stolen, the social life of London drained his resources and he threatened to turn to crime. The correspondence ended as he sought employment in Europe as a soldier of fortune under Sir William Zouche at Brabant.

To sweeten the bitter pill of imminent insolvency Henry used to add a final paragraph of the latest London news or gossip. At the end of a letter written on 4 July 1613, after discoursing on the subject of beaver hats, he appended his usual postscript.

'On tewsday last there was acted at the Globe a new play called all is triewe, which had beene acted not passing 2 or 3 times before there came many people to see it in so much that ye howse was very full and as the play was almost ended the house was fired with shooting off a Chamber which was stopt with towe which was blown up into the thetch of the house and so burnt downe to the ground but the people escaped all without hurte except one man who was scalded with the fier by

The letter sent on 4 July 1613 by Henry Bluett from London to his uncle, Richard Weekes, at Wiveliscombe. He notes the dispatch of two beaver hats and bands, promising the delivery of two Bibles and other books from Mr Lownes. He gives news of his patroness, Lady Bond, sick of 'an ague' for three or four days, whose servant, John Withy, had left her, being 'one of the beastlyest drunkeards in the Cittie'. Almost as an afterthought, he then describes the burning down of the Globe Theatre, ending 'Your dutifull nephew to dispose of, Henry Bluett'.

adventuringe in to save a Child which otherwise had beene burnte.'

There is only one other account of the burning of Shakespeare's Globe Theatre, which adds the information that the injured man had his breeches set on fire but extinguished his problem with bottled ale. There is also only one other authority for the name of the play 'All is True': the alternative title of Shakespeare's *Henry VIII*.

Original documents relating to Shakespearian drama are both rare and highly prized. Our depositor, on hearing of the discovery among his archives, withdrew the letter (after we had carefully taken a photocopy of it) and entered it for sale at Sotheby's in July 1986. I cannot in all conscience blame him, for he has left us with the remainder of his superb 200-box collection. The whole bundle of Bluett letters if sold on the open market might fetch some £400. Because of its dramatic postscript that single sheet induced an American dealer to part with a grand total of £14,000.

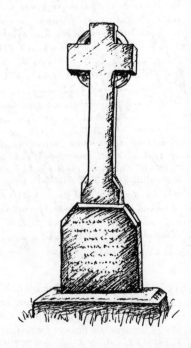

Delayed-action memorial to Charles Capell Hardwicke at Congresbury, set up in 1871.

6

THE HIGHWAYMAN AND THE GRAZIER

IN Congresbury churchyard stands a large marble monument set up by
his friends to the memory of Charles Capell Hardwicke in 1871, long
after his death in 1849 at the age of 50. Hardwicke was not even buried
at Congresbury but at Hutton. The story behind the stone is narrated
briefly in its inscription. 'He was', stated his friends, 'of such courage,
that being attacked by a highwayman on the heath in this Parish October 21st 1830 and fearfully wounded by him, he pursued his assailant
and, having overtaken him in the centre of this village, delivered him to
justice'. An appropriate verse from the Psalms was added: 'Thou shalt
not be afraid for any terror by night, nor for the arrow that flieth by
day'.

Charles Capell Hardwicke was a grazier, then living at Huish in Congresbury and acting as agent to a wool company. On the Thursday
in question he had been at Bristol market and left at six in the evening to ride home, having the very considerable sum of £450 in his
pocket. When nearly halfway back at Newlands Hatch he met a stranger
who was also on horseback, who asked if he might accompany him.
Shortly after passing through Congresbury village, at an enclosed common called the Heath, the stranger dropped back a little. Let Hardwicke
himself tell what ensued, as he did at the trial which ensued at Taunton's
Lent Assizes.

'I felt myself violently struck on the left shoulder and heard the report
as if of a pistol, and saw at the same time a flash of light close behind
me on my left side. My horse sprung forward and I cried out to the
prisoner "Good God, what have you done?" or something to that effect,
and immediately pulling my horse, I faced the prisoner, who thereupon
turned about and started away back at full gallop... As soon as the
prisoner fled I instantly pursued him, and came up with him about half a
mile from where I had been struck...I received several blows upon the
head with what I thought to be a bludgeon, and which nearly knocked
me off my horse. When I recovered from the effects of the blows, he had
got some yards farther a-head; I pursued him again and got near him a

second time, when he threatened me in some words which I did not understand. I called out to some persons who were on the road to stop him, and continued to pursue him along what is called the Kent-road. There was a cart on the road, by which the prisoner attempted to pass on the right side, I being on the left a little behind. The way by the right side of the cart being too narrow, he turned his horse into the middle of the road, and the horse fell in attempting to make the short turn. I had come up with him at that instant, and in the same moment my horse also fell. As soon as I got upon my legs again, I caught hold of the prisoner, and a struggle took place between us. In the struggle I felt pierced in my left side, and afterwards received several violent blows on the head...My hat had fallen off when my horse fell, and one of the blows upon the head so stunned me that I let the prisoner go. He then got upon his horse, and was on the point of again riding away, when I found that I had sufficiently recovered to be able to seize the bridle. Whilst I held the bridle he attempted to strike me with his fist, having, as I suppose, dropped the weapon in the scuffle. Whilst I had a hold of him some persons came up, and we took him to the inn at Congresbury.'

Hardwicke's determination, despite his wounds, is the more incredible when considering his physical stature compared with that of his assailant. Hardwicke was described as 'a slight man, under the middle height, and exhibits no appearance whatever of a muscular conformation; and showed, as it seemed, a remarkably delicate structure about the shoulders and breast'. The highwayman, on the other hand, was 'a stout built man, above the middle size, well set, with a broad chest, strong shoulders, and all appearances of possessing great muscular power'. He was also armed with a double-barrelled pistol and a stick loaded at one end with lead, through which he could shoot out an eight-inch dagger on a spring, which he used to stab his victim through the lung.

The ruthless highwayman was 37-year-old Richard Hewlett, a tanner, born at Wick St Lawrence and formerly a smallholder near Huish at Congresbury. He had been in the habit of attending fairs at Binegar and elsewhere, apparently for the purchase of horses but in reality to conspire with 'desperate characters engaged in the practice of horse-stealing'. Five years before he had been accused of such a theft and obtained £50 from a relation on promising to emigrate to America. After a short while, however, he reappeared. He was married, literate and had three children.

Hewlett's Assize trial lasted seven hours although the jury took almost no time at all to find him guilty. Mr Justice Parke sentenced him to death, which the prisoner greeted 'with all the mock heroism of a hardened desperado, who was careless alike of life, death, and eternity; and he left the dock bowing to the Judge with the flippancy of an unconcerned spectator'. The Judge praised Hardwicke's courage and awarded him £30 over and above his costs.

We can turn up the Ilchester Gaol description book, used to record the physical appearance of prisoners before the discovery of photography in case of escape. This adds the information that Hewlett was 5ft 10¼ins tall, of smart person, with a sallow complexion, oval face, sandy hair, hazel eyes and having scars on his forehead and his left cheek. He apparently nursed hopes of a reprieve right up to the arrival of the mail on his execution day, 22 April 1831, although after the public reaction to Hardwicke's fortitude any such hopes were doomed to disappointment. With the realisation of his impending fate his nerve seemed to fail him and he asked Mr Hardy, the gaoler, for a glass of wine. At Hewlett's request he was attended on his last day by a Yeovil dissenting minister, Mr Jukes, but he refused to confess his guilt, although hinting mysteriously that infidelity was the cause of his downfall. The final procession assembled at 11.20 led by the executioner, who was followed by the prisoner, two clergymen, the Under Sheriff and Mr Hardy.

The reporter from the *Western Flying Post* was there to describe the scene for his readers. 'The miserable man passed along with a firm step; his countenance was pale as death, but it bore a determined and unprepossessing appearance. On passing the prisoners in the court he turned, as if wishing to speak, but walked on without doing so. Having arrived at the drop, he shook hands with those who followed him, and then knelt and appeared to pray fervently with Mr Jukes, who at his request addressed the spectators, and desired that they would take warning by the present example. The prisoner desired that a little time might be allowed him; and after the expiration of a few seconds, when everything was adjusted, he resolutely threw the handkerchief from him, and was launched – fearfully – awfully, into eternity. His struggles could scarcely be observed – to those who were near him they appeared to continue about five minutes. His body remained the usual time and was then cut down and buried the same evening.'

Thus ended the story behind the monument in Congresbury churchyard. The puzzle as to why Hardwicke's friends waited 22 years after his death and a full 41 years after the event to commemorate his bravery remains a mystery.

7

THE ENMORE EFFIGIES

WILLS are fascinating documents. They provide for or deprive, raise or dash hopes, and represent the only real means by which people can extend their wishes and their influence beyond the grave. We are less blessed in Somerset, for virtually all wills proved in the various church courts of the diocese of Bath and Wells were destroyed by German bombing at Exeter in 1942, during the Second World War.

One will which has fortunately come down to us was made in 1779 by Jasper Porter of Bloxham in Enmore, who died in 1781. The bulk of his estates, including considerable property in Enmore, Broomfield and Spaxton, he left to his daughter Susanna. To his son Jasper he left merely a leasehold interest in lands at Bridgwater and to his son Thomas a small estate at Woolavington.

The two sons were understandably distraught at being, as they saw it, disinherited by their father. There survives a letter written in 1784 by Dr Jasper Porter from Barnstaple to his younger brother Thomas, then a sugar planter at Demerara in the West Indies. This shows that their sister withheld even the title deeds to the small properties left to the brothers. Jasper expressed himself 'extremely sorry to find your circumstances almost as deplorable as my own but, as we are brothers in affliction as well as consanguinity, I shall no longer dwell on the melancholy picture of our present situation or reflect on the baseness of a sister's conduct which can only exasperate our sense of misfortune without alleviating it'. He had clearly swallowed a dictionary.

Jasper urged his brother to return to England to join with him in a Chancery suit against their sister following 'the Old Rogue's death'. To add insult to injury, their sister had not only married and been recently delivered of a son but, 'by way of farce to the comedy, compliments and congratulations have been sent to me by Mr Crosse', the new brother-in-law.

Dr Jasper Porter later moved to Little Deane in Gloucestershire but he neither forgot nor forgave. By his own will of 1795 he set aside £30 to put up a marble bust of himself with a Latin inscription to extol his many virtues. The bulk of the will, however, was taken up with an incredible series of provisions:

'In consequence of being defrauded of my birthright and paternal estate by the cruel and unnatural will of my father in 1779, which was effected by the villainy and artifice of my sister to aggrandize her fortune and become his executrix, I would stigmatize their memory to latest posterity and exhibit a picture of them in full length, that I may deter the vicious from acts of injustice which disgrace humanity, and assure the world that the memory of bad actions can be only effaced by public marks of detestation and abhorrence. Wherefore my will is that £10 be deposited in the hands of the Overseers of the Parish of Enmore, which they shall distribute equally amongst ten of the oldest men paupers of the said Parish, on condition that on the 5th day of November they make two effigies, representing a man and a woman, which shall be fixed on two stakes and a copy of my father's will shall be affixed thereto with a label in large characters of these words.

"To expiate the crimes of fraud and perfidy and make some atonement to the manes of the testator, we commit this effigy to the flames at the request and in commemoration of our benefactor".

'The ten men shall assemble at the Castle Inn at Enmore and walk in

St Michael's Church, Enmore, outside which Dr Jasper Porter posthumously and vainly required his father and sister to be annually burned in effigy.

slow procession at the beat of the drum through the village and carry the above effigies, with my father's will affixed thereto, as far as the great elm near the Church, when a bonfire shall be provided for burning the effigies. The oldest of the ten men on arriving at the place shall then commit the said effigies to the flames and in a solemn and audible voice first repeat these words. "To expiate the frauds and perfidy and make some atonement to the manes of the Testator, we commit these effigies to the flames at the request and in commemoration of our benefactor."

'After performing the ceremony the men shall repair to the Castle Inn at dinner and there receive the £10 divided amongst them agreeable to the words of my will on the 5th day of November every year, provided that they perform the ceremony of burning the said effigies in the manner above recited.'

Try as I might, I have been unable to find any evidence that the ceremony was ever performed. If Jasper's sister had been able to accomplish even half the crimes of which he accused her, she must have had little difficulty in frustrating his ludicrous legacy.

Andrew Crosse of Fyne Court, Broomfield (1784-1855), the experimental electrician of the Quantocks and son of the grasping Susanna.

[34]

As a footnote to the whole affair, the Mr Crosse whom Susanna married was Richard Crosse of Fyne Court in neighbouring Broomfield, and the son that she produced in 1784 was the celebrated Andrew Crosse. Richard Crosse died when Andrew was only 16 and he was brought up by his doting mother, Susanna. Andrew went on to become a pioneer in the study of electricity. Among the Quantock people he was known as 'the Thunder and Lightning Man' who subsequently believed that he had created life, in the form of insects of an unrecorded genus which crawled out of stones through which he had passed electric current. The poet, Percy Bysshe Shelley, and his wife Mary attended one of Crosse's London lectures in 1814 and some commentators believe that it was then that Mary Shelley got the idea for the character of Frankenstein. Indeed the latest biography of Andrew Crosse was entitled *The Man who was Frankenstein*.

With what we already know of Susanna Crosse, I think she would have been highly amused.

8

AUDACIOUS AVALON

THE belief that Glastonbury Abbey was founded soon after the Crucifixion by St Joseph of Arimathea, that his staff, planted in the ground there, grew into the Holy Thorn, and that King Arthur and his Queen Guinevere were buried within the abbey precinct, bring thousands to the town each year. Many better-qualified writers than myself have commented on these stories, but they have had precious little effect on the popular mind. On the grounds that constant dripping may conceivably begin to wear away a stone, it cannot be repeated too often that there is no historical or archaeological evidence whatsoever to support such tales. Even more ludicrous is the incredible claim that the figures of the Zodiac and other creatures can be discerned in the landscape around Glastonbury and that these had been constructed by 2000 BC to form a 'Temple of the Stars'.

The St Joseph saga was invented at Glastonbury, probably in the 13th century, to challenge Westminster Abbey's assertion that their foundation was older than the Somerset monastery. In those days precedence was just as important in the ecclesiastical world as it was in the secular. The Arthurian accounts began a little earlier, apparently inspired by the need to encourage pilgrims with their money to come to Glastonbury in order to fund the rebuilding of the Abbey after it had burned down in 1184. The Zodiac was the brainchild of Katherine Maltwood and had no existence before her first book on the subject, published in 1935.

There is no evidence, either from excavations or contemporary documents, that the abbey at Glastonbury is any older than about 670, from which time reliable charters begin to survive, indicating the patronage of successive kings of Wessex. Inscriptions which survived into the 12th century may provide the names of some earlier abbots, but their chronology is far from clear. References which suggest that St Patrick ended his

The hallowed precinct of Glastonbury Abbey as seen in 1723 by William Stukeley. The Abbot's Lodgings to the right of the engraving had then recently been demolished but were depicted from an earlier drawing.

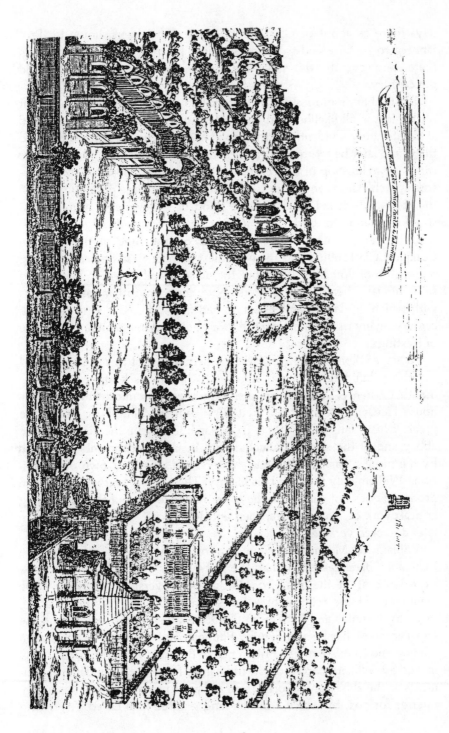

days there as abbot of Glastonbury c. 460 have been shown by Prof Finberg to be false and to relate probably to another Patrick (of which there were several), who may have been buried there as late as the mid 9th century.

Glastonbury's glories began largely with St Dunstan, born near that settlement, in all likelihood at Baltonsborough, in 909. He was educated at Glastonbury, evidently at the hands of Irish scholars who had settled there, and later he returned there as abbot, before embarking on a further career as archbishop of Canterbury. Indeed five of Dunstan's six successors as archbishop came from Glastonbury. It was these potent links with the abbey which led to a veritable flood of endowments from successive kings and the burial of three of them, Edmund, Edgar and Edmund Ironside, within the abbey itself. By the time of the Norman Conquest Glastonbury was the wealthiest monastery in England, owning one eighth of Somerset alone, but the place lacked a written heritage to set it similarly head and shoulders above the many other Saxon abbeys with which England was blessed. It had also suffered during the 11th century: many of its lands granted away both before and after the Battle of Hastings.

Henry of Blois, nephew of Henry I, became abbot in 1126 and found the abbey buildings in a sad state with the monks leading a hand-to-mouth existence. Apart from restoring the economic fortunes of his house, Henry appears to have invited William of Malmesbury, one of the greatest historians of that time, to research and write the history of the abbey and of the saints connected with it. Using documents preserved by the monks, particularly their charters, and also their own oral traditions, William duly produced his history. The original text which William produced does not survive in the form that he left it, but the painstaking critical work of Antonia Gransden and John Scott has restored it from later doctored versions.

William of Malmesbury, drawing on an story recounted by the Venerable Bede, asserted that the abbey was founded by two missionaries sent in the year 167 (or in other versions, 156) by Pope Eleutherius at the request of a British King, Lucius. This information, taken by Nennius and Bede from the 6th century *Liber Pontificalis* in the Papal archives, has been shown by Plummer and others to be a mistaken reading and to relate not to Britain but to Britium (Birtha) at Edessa, now in Turkey. William copied down the names from certain undated monuments at the abbey and quoted from a charter he dated as 601, probably in error for 701, by which a British king granted land called Ynyswitrin to Glastonbury. Ynyswitrin was later seized on as an older name for Glastonbury itself, although Finberg has shown that it is likely to have been an estate in Cornwall.

William's work proved less than satisfactory in the eyes of the monks and in the 13th century, principally in about 1230 and 1247, substantial additions were made to the history. For the first time the disciples supposedly sent by Eleutherius were named as Phagan and Deruvian (probably derived from Geoffrey of Monmouth's pseudo-history), but, more significantly, it was stated that in 63 AD St Philip, preaching in Gaul, sent twelve of his disciples, led by St Joseph of Arimathea, who settled at Glastonbury alias Ynyswitrin. From this point the legends began to snowball.

Surprisingly, the Holy Thorn appeared on the scene much later: indeed, only shortly before the abbey was dissolved. A life of St Joseph, printed in 1520, speaks of three hawthorns on Wirrall Hill which 'do burge and bere grene leaves at Christmas', but the link with Joseph and his staff was not drawn until as recently as the early 18th century. I have found no evidence that the tradition of sending a flowering sprig to the monarch at Christmas, claimed to have been practised since 'olden days', is a custom any earlier than the time of George V.

William of Malmesbury also wrote a history of the kings of England. The fact that none of the later additions to his Glastonbury work feature in his more general treatise is yet another indication that they are not from his pen.

The connection between Glastonbury and Arthur was first alleged in the 12th century. Without any question it arose from the tragic gutting of the abbey by fire on 25 May 1184, a fire which destroyed not only most of its buildings but also all the documents on which William of Malmesbury had laboured some fifty years before. The monks' most fruitful source of finance, the Crown, had also been threatened by the death of their most generous patron, Henry II, in 1189. At that time, thanks to the over-imaginative History of the Britons by Geoffrey of Monmouth, c. 1138, the name of Arthur was on all lips and the growth of legends around his person had already begun. If the monks had had to choose a hitherto unknown grave to dig up which would bring in both the pilgrims and the money to rebuild the abbey, they could not have found a better 12th-century candidate than Arthur.

Geoffrey of Monmouth had described Arthur's burial on the Isle of Avalon, an 'otherworld' across the water without any precise geographical location, where Arthur's sword was also forged. All the monks had to do in 1191 was to engineer the discovery of the grave and provide evidence that identified Glastonbury with Avalon. The monks carefully screened off the site with curtains, in the style of a medieval Paul Daniels, before producing the 'king' and 'queen', together with an inscribed leaden cross which completed the Glastonbury-Avalon equation. Continuing a theme initiated by Chretien de Troyes, Robert de Boron, a Burgundian poet, added the Holy Grail to the legend in the early 13th century. It was Robert who identified it as both the cup of the Last Supper and the vessel in which St Joseph collected Christ's blood, before taking it to Avalon. Indeed, it may well have been Robert's work which in turn prompted the monks of Glastonbury to adopt St Joseph in the first place.

Other elements in the Glastonbury myth are comparatively modern: the story that Christ and the Virgin Mary visited the place and that the Grail was buried in the vicinity of Chalice Well. The well was apparently formerly called Chalkwell and the name survives in the nearby Chilkwell Street in Glastonbury. Just as modern is the preposterous theory of the Glastonbury Zodiac.

In 1935 Katherine Maltwood, a sculptress and illustrator, in her book *A Guide to Glastonbury's Temple of the Stars*, claimed to have traced on Ordnance Survey maps the outlines of the Zodiac figures in the landscape of the Somerset Levels to the south and east of Glastonbury. Further, she asserted that these figures corresponded to the relative positions of their constellations in the sky and also that her 'temple' had been created by prehistoric man in either 2700 BC (1935) or 2000 BC (1937).

The multiplicity of lines on an English Ordnance map makes it possible to construct almost any design one chooses. Even so, Mrs Maltwood found it necessary to amend some of her Zodiac signs, so that Libra became the Dove, Aquarius the Phoenix, and Cancer Argo (the Ship), and even to add the figures of Cetus (the Whale) and, to 'guard' the Temple from the south-west, the 'Girt Dog of Langport', otherwise termed 'the Questing Beast' or 'Canis Major'.

In 1983 Somerset archaeologist Dr Ian Burrow examined Katherine Maltwood's figures, comparing their outlines with old maps of the Levels. He showed quite clearly that many of the lines were wishful thinking and entirely arbitrary, and that others were established by features which were of comparatively modern origin. He found that Cancer/Argo was almost entirely defined by droves and drainage ditches laid out by Inclosure Awards between 1798 and 1829. Leo's foreleg was formed by a road diversion made necessary by a railway built in only 1905, and his muzzle and mouth by modern woodland tracks. The Phoenix's left wing was delineated by a turnpike road constructed between 1782 and 1800, where no road had run before, while Capricorn's eye was located only by an ephemeral haystack which Mrs Maltwood mistook for a permanent feature on an aerial photograph.

I am well aware that I have brought little new to the Glastonbury saga but I hope that I may have encouraged others to look more critically at the incredibly tall stories purveyed in a host of well-meaning but misguided publications.

9

MANCHESTER JACK

IN 1985 the Somerset Record Office received an enquiry from Mr Mark Sorell of Essex, who was researching for a book on travelling shows. He had tracked down in an out-of-the-way book, *Soldiering and Scribbling* by Archibald Forbes, published in 1872, a cursory account of England's first great lion tamer. It ran as follows:

'Who was the first lion-king in this country? Well, sir, I can tell you all about them, and, in fact, the whole story about menageries. The first great menagerie proprietor I ever heard anything on was old Wombwell, who was originally a shoemaker in the Commercial Road, and who first travelled about with a big serpent. Before ever Van Amberg a great American lion-tamer was heard on, old "Manchester Jack" was doing the lion-king in one of Wombwell's travelling menageries, well on to fifty year ago. The manager, I remember well his name, was Bromsgrove. He was a better man, was Manchester Jack, than Van Amberg; they were to have had a regular competition once at Southampton, and lots of money was betted over the matter; but before the time came the American funked on it, and would not come on. Jack took to hotel-keeping in Taunton, with Bromsgrove for head waiter, and died within the last seven years.'

The problem, posed by Mr Sorell, was how to identify Manchester Jack without a definite Christian name and certainly no surname to search for. James Bromsgrove (c.1798-1852) was a butcher who at one time had his own travelling menagerie and was also the exhibitor of a blind 'giant', Joseph Neal Sewell. Sewell had arrived at Taunton from Swansea in about 1825 and Bromsgrove, with a suitable caravan, had taken him down to Exeter and continued to travel around until Sewell died in 1829, aged only 23, and was buried at St Mary's in Taunton.

In 1843 Bromsgrove became tenant of the Halfway House, now the Harp Inn, Shoreditch Road, in Taunton and was remembered as having accommodated his 'retired' circus animals in cages behind the inn which kept the locals awake with their roaring. His son, John Bromsgrove, could also have been the friend of Manchester Jack mentioned by Forbes.

The Church of St Mary Magdalene, Taunton: a 19th century engraving from an 18th century original. Here the blind giant, Joseph Neal Sewell, was buried and 'Manchester Jack' was married.

John was a carpenter by trade but succeeded his father at the Halfway House on James's death in 1852. In 1854 he married Sarah Caines, an engineer's daughter, and the pair became tenants of local brewer, William Ellis Oram, at the Four Alls Inn. This still stands, although rebuilt, at the corner of Bath Place and Corporation Street. In 1861-2 John and his wife bought the nearby Winchester Arms on Castle Green which they ran together until John's death in 1866, aged only 37. His widow, Sarah, continued as landlady until she too died in 1877, and was followed by her daughter, Elizabeth.

None of this helped to identify Manchester Jack, for neither the Census Returns of 1851 nor those of 1861 showed any possible candidate as living with the Bromsgroves. The only non family member at the Halfway House in 1851 was Nathaniel Farnham, then described as an ostler aged 46. Intriguingly Farnham indirectly added to the saga. A contemporary description of the funeral of Sewell the giant referred to 'a

Somersetshire dwarf named Farnham, only 37 inches high,' who followed the coffin as chief mourner and had apparently been exhibited with Sewell to make the latter appear even taller. Farnham had been baptised at Misterton near Crewkerne on 6 September 1807 and is clearly to be identified with 'Nat', ostler at the Phoenix Inn, East Street, Taunton, referred to by the *Somerset County Herald* as having died on 1 August 1868, 'formerly the dwarf in Wombwell's menagerie'. St Mary's parish register duly records the burial of Nathaniel Farnham on 2 August 1868 aged 69 (sic).

I was still no nearer to identifying the famous Manchester Jack, however, until Mr Sorell wrote again in March 1987. He suggested searching the 1861 Census Returns for all Taunton publicans shown with Christian names of John, James, Jack or J. in *Kelly's Directory of Somerset* of that year. Archivists do not normally have the time to devote to such protracted research on behalf of correspondents but on this occasion my curiosity had been well and truly roused. To my delight the search finally threw up a possible candidate in the shape of John Gill, innkeeper at the Phoenix Inn, aged 51, born at Salford, Lancashire, and also employer of the dwarf, Nat Farnham.

Further research provided independent confirmation. John Gill, innkeeper, son of Henry Gill, labourer, was married at St Mary's to Betsy Bromsgrove, daughter of James Bromsgrove, innkeeper, on 7 May 1844. In that year, shortly before his wedding, Gill had taken over the Royal Marine Inn, Silver Street, as tenant of Mr Oram. The couple continued there until 1855 when they moved to the Phoenix. They had no fewer than nine children baptised in Taunton, between 1845 and 1861, and at the baptisms of three of these the father was described as John Manchester Gill. *The Taunton Courier* recorded the death on 26 February 1865 at the Phoenix Tavern of 'Mr John Manchester Gill, after a painful illness, aged 55, deeply regretted by a large circle of friends'. His widow Betsy continued at the Phoenix until she left in 1869-70.

Manchester Jack had been finally run to earth.

10

THE INCESTUOUS BARONET

IN the parish of Curry Rivel on the main road from Taunton to Langport lie the house and estate of Burton Pynsent. The most prominent feature on the property is a Tuscan column, 140 feet tall, which the famous politician, William Pitt the Elder, later earl of Chatham, set up to the memory of Sir William Pynsent. Sir William, who died in 1765 without surviving issue, left his entire Burton estate to Pitt. Recent publications have pronounced that Pynsent's reasons for making the bequest were founded on Somerset's reaction to the hated Cider Tax, the story of which is told in another chapter.

Thus, in the county guide-book issued by the Somerset County Council in 1986 the Pynsent column is illustrated and the statement is made that 'it may be regarded as Somerset's Monument to Cider Drinking' because Pynsent made his bequest as a result of 'Pitt's opposition to a proposed tax on cider'. The story is repeated in Enid Byfield's *Somerset Curiosities,* published in 1987. Unfortunately the facts do not support this contention.

Sir William Pynsent, second Baronet from Urchfont in Wiltshire, married the heir to the Burton estate in Curry Rivel, Mary daughter of Thomas Jennings and widow of Edmund Star. Thereupon he quitted Wiltshire and moved to Burton to enjoy his wife's inheritance, serving as Whig Member of Parliament for Taunton from 1715 until 1722. He continued to exercise a Whig influence in local Parliamentary politics, supporting Sir Charles Wyndham at Taunton in 1734 and Bubb Doddington at Bridgwater in 1741.

Pynsent's wife died before him, as did his only son and three daughters. Mrs Barrington, in her biography of the economist Walter Bagehot, described Pynsent thus: 'His manners were eccentric, his morals lay under odious imputations, but his fidelity to his political opinions were unalterable'. Horace Walpole stated that 'he had parts and humour, not many scruples, living to her death with his only daughter in pretty notorious incest'. This daughter, Leonora Ann, passed away on 12 October 1763. Only eight days later, probably still suffering from the

grief of his loss, Pynsent drew up his will leaving his lands at Burton to Pitt and relatively minor bequests to members of his family. It was a will that he never revoked. No hint of the reason for the bequest was contained in the will, Pynsent commenting only that 'I hope he will like my Burton Estate where I now live well enough to make it his Country Seat'. *The Western Flying Post*, a week after Pynsent's death on 8 January 1765 aged 85, remarked that the motive for his munificence towards Pitt, 'though he had never seen him', resulted 'solely from his being of opinion that he [Pitt] is a good patriot and wishes well to his country'.

According to Arthur Mounter's *Social History of Curry Rivel in the 19th century*, Pynsent's lawyer, Elias Bamfield, rode to London on horseback to break the glad tidings to Pitt. Unfortunately he arrived so late at night and in such a disshevelled state that Pitt at first refused to see him. It was with difficulty that Banfield persuaded his way into Pitt's presence and told him of his good fortune. It was only five months after Pynsent's death that Pitt arrived at Curry Rivel in great state and made his home at Burton.

It is, however, impossible that Pynsent's bequest could have been inspired by Pitt's opposition to the hated cider tax. Pynsent's will was dated, as we have seen, in October 1763 and Pitt is not known to have opposed the tax until October 1764, later seconding the motion for the tax's repeal in March 1766. It is yet another of those Somerset stories which simply will not bear close examination. It is also ironic that one of this county's best-known monuments should have been set up by a famous statesman to the memory of an incestuous bigot.

(Opposite): *Burton Pynsent, from an engraving of 1785, showing the house after William Pitt constructed an additional range. The Pynsent monument, reputedly designed by Lancelot 'Capability' Brown in 1765, crowns the ridge to the left.*

11
ONE WOMAN'S LEGS

A FLAT stone, formerly in Saltford churchyard near Bath and now in the church porch behind an umbrella stand, bears a very curious inscription:

> Stop Reader, and a Wonder See,
>   As strange as e'er was known!
> My Feet drop'd off from my Body,
>   In the Middle of the Bone.
> I had no Surgeon for my Help
>   But God Almighty's Aid,
> In Whom I ever will rely
>   And never be afraid.
> Though here beneath Intred [interred] they lie
>   Corruption for to see,
> Yet they shall one Day reunite
>   To all Eternity.
>   Francis Flood April 1 1723

From the date of the inscription it might be thought that the stone was intended as some sort of joke. The background to this strange epitaph, however, is contained in a short and rare tract entitled *The Devonshire Woman: or a Wonderful Narrative of Frances Flood'* being 'Printed for Frances Flood, and sold by Nobody but herself'.

Frances Flood was apparently born at Gittisham near Honiton in Devon and in 1723, at the age of 32, travelled from Norton St Philip to Saltford and took lodging at an inn. The following morning she got up -

'but being come out of the door, I was taken very ill and, before I came to the village I was not sensible in what condition I was in and not able to go, was forced to hold by the wall as I went along. With great difficulty I got to the Overseer's house and desired him to get me a lodging, but he denied me; whereupon I went up the street and lay in a hogstye, where many people came to see me. I lay there till the evening in a sad condition, when the Overseer's wife of that place led me to the Overseer's again, but he still denied me relief and, not being very sensible, I returned again to the same place, but they had been so inhuman as to put some dung into it to prevent my lodging there again; but at last I got into another which had no cover over it as the other had. In the morning when I awoke, I went up the street and with weakness fell down, so that streams of water ran over me, till helped up by the Clerk of the parish's wife, who led me till I came to the wall, by which I held, and with great trouble got to the barn, but the owner of the barn was so barbarous as to unhang the door the next day. A young man, out of compassion, hung the door again. The owner was so displeased that he came a second time and unhung it.'

At this point I should perhaps pause and suggest that only those with strong stomachs should read on.

'The next day the small-pox appeared on me and was noised about; insomuch that the Overseer came and put up the door, and then I had both meat and drink, but took no further care of me for 14 days. The small-pox appeared very kind and favourable and might have done very well, had I not been taken in my legs and should have been able to go away in a fortnight. After which I was taken on my calfs, which turned black and cold and looked much like scalds, and broke out. I applied to them first of all a bathe, but the flesh speedily parted from the small of my legs to the bones. I had there by me some ointment, which was brought me by the Overseer; but had no one to dress my wounds but did all myself.'

If this sounds bad enough, it was to get worse.

'My pains increased to a wonderful degree and my legs grew worse, and was driven to dismal extremity, and lay in that condition three weeks. On the 18th day of March about 8 o'clock in the evening there came a woman to the barn-door to ask me how I did. I was going to show her how my legs were and how the flesh was separated from the bones and, leaning a little harder than ordinary upon my left leg, it broke off as though it were a rotten stick a little below the calf. The woman left me, and I was surprised, but God enabled me to bind up my leg again with the same medicines as before. And when most of the people of the village were at rest, then a man that liv'd over against the barn came to see me and asked me how I did. I desired him to get me some beer at the Overseer's, but he fetched me some of his own and left me; so that there was no one with me. I submitted myself to God and, after some time, fell asleep and slept till the morning. And as soon as 'twas light, dressed the wound before any came to me, and the flesh covered the bone, but had no loss of marrow and but little of

[49]

blood, nor hardly any pain.

I was visited by abundance of people, and amongst them God sent me the Minister of Keinsham, and Mr Brown of the same town came along with him, and they afforded me much comfort. They told me they never saw the like, and it was God's handy work and not man's. So taking leave of me, they wished that the God of Heaven might be my physician, and it gave me a merry heart and cheerful countenance, and gave them thanks for what favours I had received from them, and my pains still ceased.

Abundance came both far and near all the week to see me, and amongst the rest a surgeon, who persuaded me to have the bone of my right leg taken off, to which I gave consent.

On the 25th about 6 in the morning, when I arose and opened the cloaths, I found my legs were fallen from me, and the pains I then suffered were not worthy to be called pains. So I dressed it with the same medicine I made use of before. Within two hours after came several people to visit me. I unbound the cloaths and the flesh was closed over the bone and the blood was stopp'd. So I had great reason to praise the Lord for all His mercies and favours I had received from time to time.'

The story is an incredible one: more incredible for the sentiments of deliverance expressed by the unfortunate woman. It was evidently printed for Frances to hawk around while she travelled the country on crutches. Most incredible, however, is the fact that the Saltford parishioners would not only gather up the detached and mutilated limbs and solemnly inter them in their churchyard, but also mark the spot with a gravestone complete with its gruesome inscription.

[50]

12

THE HEAVENLY CANNONBALL

AT the western end of the parish of Stogumber, near the village of
Monksilver and below the Brendon Hills, stands the Tudor mansion of Combe Sydenham Hall. It can possibly be identified with an
estate called Combe held by the Saxon Ailmer at the time of the Norman Conquest and was evidently the property which was acquired in
1367 by a judge, Richard Sydenham, who died in 1403. It continued
in the Sydenham family, apart from a short hiatus during Cromwell's
Commonwealth, until sold by Sir John Posthumous Sydenham in 1693.
The present building, which incorporates certain medieval fragments, is
largely Elizabethan, bearing the date 1580 and the initials of Sir George
Sydenham.

It was Sir George's daughter, Elizabeth, who was to become the most
noted member of her family as the second wife of Sir Francis Drake. The
story of that marriage has often been told, and recently has been given
renewed life in the Rev Alan Holt's *West Somerset* (1984), Sally Jones's
Mysteries in the Somerset Landscape (1986) and Sally Norris's *Tales of Old
Somerset* (1989).

According to these works (and many others) Sir Francis Drake, following the death of his first wife, wooed and won Elizabeth, despite the
wishes of her parents that she should marry Sir William Courtenay of
Powderham Castle in Devon. Before the couple could be married, Drake
had to depart on a lengthy sea voyage and, after several years of wait-
ing, Elizabeth was persuaded that he had been lost at sea and that she
should marry Sir William. On her very wedding day at Stogumber, while
on her way up the church path, a cannonball (or meteorite) fell from the
skies and crashed at Elizabeth's feet. Convinced that this was a sign from
Drake, even a cannonball fired from his ship, she cried out 'that's my
Frankie !', or words to that effect, turned on her heel and hurried back to
Combe Sydenham to await her beloved. He eventually returned and she
duly became Lady Drake at Stogumber Church on 8 February 1585. The
happy couple continued together, living at Buckland Abbey in Devon,
until Drake's death at sea in 1596. Thereafter Elizabeth married the man

her father had intended for her, Sir William Courtenay. To add credence to the story, the very cannonball (or meteorite) is preserved at Combe Sydenham to this day.

The story is at least as old as 1810, when it featured in 'Combe Sydenham or the Magic Ball', a 30-verse poem published by James Jennings of Huntspill. In this earliest version Drake, his suit to the fair Elinor (as Elizabeth was referred to in the poem) rejected by her father, eloped with the girl and married her. The voyage which took him from her bed for two years was placed after the celebration of their nuptials, not before, and the cannonball rolled into Combe Sydenham courtyard to prevent a bigamous union. The missile, resting in that same courtyard in 1810 and weighing 103 lb, was credited with always returning thence whenever moved. Subsequent accounts indicate that by 1897 the cannonball had been moved into the hall of the house, kept under the table and was noted to roll up and down to presage a death in the family. It spent some time incarcerated in the County Museum in Taunton Castle, until reclaimed by the present owner of Combe Sydenham, Mr William Theed, and can still be seen exhibited in the house today.

Unfortunately hardly any of the elements in the tale, as retailed in more recent times, will bear examination. Drake married his first wife, Mary Newman, at St Budeaux Church, Plymouth, on 4 July 1569 and buried her in the churchyard there on 25 January 1583. Drake's second marriage to Elizabeth Sydenham is usually dated to 1585, apparently on the evidence of their marriage settlement, a document executed on 10 February of that year. The deed states that the marriage had already been solemnized, but gives no indication as to how long before this had taken place. On Elizabeth's portrait at Buckland Abbey the date of the marriage is given as 1584, but in fact the wedding took place even earlier, on 18 June 1583.

The venue could not possibly have been Stogumber Church. The parish registers survive for the period and contain no record of the ceremony. The only other neighbouring church, Monksilver, has lost its registers for the relevant years but fortunately the volume recording the marriage was extant in 1717 when the text of the entry was extracted by Philip Sydenham of Combe Sydenham and sent in a letter to an Oxford don, Mr Hunt of Balliol College:

'Sir Francis Drake, kt., and Elizabeth Sydenham, daughter of George Sydenham, were married the 18th day of June 1583 by Mr Barret, Archdeacon of Exeter.'

Thomas Barrett had been instituted Archdeacon in January 1583 and continued to hold office until his death in 1633 at the venerable age of 82. Thus Drake married Elizabeth only six months after the death of his first wife and we know from other sources that he embarked on no voyage during that time and was probably resident at Plymouth throughout the period. Indeed, some might think that Sir Francis's courtship, engagement and second marriage followed his bereavement with unseemly haste. Similarly, there is no contemporary evidence for Sir George Sydenham's displeasure at the idea of Drake as a son-in-law.

Intriguingly there is independent evidence for the 1583 date. The only other records ever found of Sir Francis's presence in Somerset relate to the same period. The Yeovil churchwardens' accounts for 1583-4 show the receipt of 1s 8d from 'Sir Francis Drake for a Peal with all the Bells'. Similarly the Bridgwater Receiver's accounts for the same year indicate that the then Mayor, Philip Holworthy, spent 19s 6d in entertaining 'Syr Franses Dracke'. Sadly, the immediate circumstances surrounding this progress, for such it appears to have been, are probably lost beyond recovery. Moreover, one of the two surviving portraits of Elizabeth Sydenham, believed originally to have come from Combe Sydenham and now at Greenwich, is dated 1583 and describes her as aged 22. It now seems likely that this was a wedding portrait. Surprisingly, John Sugden in his new biography of Drake (1990), although he cites the Sydenham letter of 1717, redates the register entry from 1583 to 1585 and then discards it as evidence.

A further point is that Sir William Courtenay was not available as an alternative suitor in 1583. He had married his first wife, another Elizabeth, the daughter of the Earl of Rutland, by special licence from the Bishop of London dated 18 January 1573. Although I have been unable to trace the date of her death, the registers of Powderham for this period having been lost and any possible memorial having been destroyed during the Civil War, Courtenay then proceeded to have ten children by her: seven sons and three daughters. He could not possibly have been free to marry Elizabeth Sydenham in 1583 or before.

The answer to the riddle is that in origin the cannonball story appears to relate not to Elizabeth Sydenham but to Drake's first wife, Mary Newman. The Devon version of the tale appeared in Robert Southey's *Lives of the Admirals* (1833) and in Mrs A.E. Bray's *The Borders of the Tamar and the Tavy* (1838), the latter book being written in the form of letters to Southey. According to the tale recounted to Mrs Bray by the Devon countryfolk, following his first marriage, Drake had been away on a voyage for seven years when his wife Mary gave him up for lost and decided to marry again. Sir Francis, on the other side of the world, was informed by 'one of his spirits' of the situation. Charging one of his great guns, he fired a cannonball 'so truly aimed that it shot right through the globe, forced its way into the church, and fell with a loud explosion between the lady and her intended bridegroom', effectively disrupting the wedding.

The variant version told to Southey claimed that 'a huge round stone fell through the air upon the train of the intended bride's gown as she was on the way to church', adding that the same stone was still used as 'a weight upon the harrow of the farm, and if it be removed from the estate in which it fell, always returns thither'.

The tale of Drake and his cannonball thus seems likely to have started as a Devonian fancy relating to his first wife, rather than to the Somerset lass with whom Sir Francis plighted his troth at Monksilver in 1583.

13
DRINK UP THEE ZYDER !

MUCH has been written about cider in Somerset. Today it is not only an extremely popular drink but bids fair to become a major element in our expanding tourist industry. Serious research, however, has largely been restricted to the 19th and 20th centuries and much more detailed work needs to be done on earlier periods.

There was one period in time, four years in the 18th century, when cider filled the newspapers and provided the major topic of conversation in the Southwest: for in 1763 there came into force a new tax on cider and perry which permitted searches of dwelling houses and infuriated the people.

The *Western Flying Post* of 25 April 1763 marked the occasion in verse.

> Some say that Old England one night in a frolic
>   Swallow'd cyder so sharp, that it gave her the cholic.
> To prevent a relapse they a nostrum provide her
>   And Excise, as an Alkali, add to to our cyder.
>
> Shall we sing now about the brown beer and the perry,
>   Which, as Moore of Moore Hall says, so oft made us merry:
> In those days of our dads (and our fathers were wise men)
>   They could 'here's to you' say without fear of excisemen.
>
> We putters-together of what we call rhymes
>   Are pleas'd when we can have a touch at the times.
> We all love to touch – but be merry and wise,
>   For tis those who are touch'd – that have touch'd up Excise.

A fortnight later at Langport a company calling themselves the AntiScotians from Cider Land performed 'a tragi-comic farce called The Apple Tree Triumphant or the Burning of the Boot'. The mood of the moment was caught by the several thousand spectators with shouts of 'Liberty and Property', 'No Excise' and 'Confusion to Evil Counsellors', with 'Huzzas that pierced the very clouds, declaring they would sooner sacrifice their very lives than preserve them in an inglorious state of bondage and misery'. The evening ended with the ringing of bells, bonfires and illuminations, and hanging and burning an effigy.

From September 1763 the local opposition began to organize itself. An afternoon meeting of gentlemen and farmers was convened at the Castle Tavern (now the Castle Hotel), Taunton, to take constitutional measures to repeal the Tax Act, and another was held in October at Taunton Castle during the Quarter Sessions. To the fury of the cider counties, the repeal of the Act was defeated in Parliament by 224 votes to 115 in February 1764. It had been vainly argued that in its first year the cider duty had raised £27,000 but had cost £16,000 to collect. Woe betide any MP from a cider county who had voted against repeal. Protest meetings continued that year, one summoned in person by Somerset's sheriff at the Fountain Inn, Taunton, and another at the Christopher Inn at Wells.

Eventually the message got through to London and in 1766 the hated tax was abolished. Celebrations of the great event began in Somerset at Bishops Lydeard on 19 May. There 'the morning was ushered in with ringing. At noon cyder was drawn through the town by horses, adorned with ribbands, together with branches of apple trees in blossom. Cyder was given plentifully to the populace, amidst several flags and colours flying, borne and displayed by the neighbouring gentlemen, with a band of several instruments of music, and the evening concluded with a ball by a vast number of gentlemen and ladies from the neighbouring parishes, and where many loyal healths were plentifully toasted round. In short, it made so polite an appearance that chearfulness was observed in the countenance of every spectator.'

The scene moved to Taunton on 28 May where 'the effigies [sic] of a certain L-----, drest in a genteel suit of clothes, was drawn to the Cornhill [now the Parade] and publickly exhibited to a great concourse of people, to whom were given five hogsheads of cyder, and between two and three hundred loaves of bread. The effigy, after it was hung on a tree, a pile of wood was erected round it; and when it had burnt some time, fell into the flames amidst the resounding acclamations of all present. A number of the country people came there on the occasion, adorn'd with garlands of flowers and other marks of festivity and joy.'

Delight was also clearly evident on the Somerset-Dorset border at Milborne Port on 5 July 1767. 'Thomas Medlycott, one of their members, gave on this joyful occasion two hogsheads of cyder, which were brought from his seat at Ven to the town cross (music playing and bells ringing), ornamented in the following manner, viz. a young apple tree in the front of the barrels. The apples and leaves thereof were gilt with gold and silver. On the barrels were wrote the words, TAX-FREE, and a man striding the barrels carried a gilt staff and frame, on which was the following inscription, "By the Providence of God and a British Parliament, Liberty was restored, July 5 1766 ". They adjourned to the Angel Inn where they drank Mr Medlycott's health, Mr Pitt's, Mr Dowdeswell's, Lord Camden's, and several other Noblemen's, the friends of Liberty; and the night was spent with a joy peculiar on so happy an occasion.'

Even a hint that a man had supported the cider tax could prove fatal to his career. One of the Somerset MPs, Charles Kemys Tynte of Halswell House near Bridgwater, suffered just such a smear campaign and was forced to publish an address to the gentlemen, clergy and freeholders of the county. Tynte described how he spoke in the House against the Act and was only absent from the debate for one day on account of a severe attack of the gout, 'that I could not turn in my bed without assistance'. He had attended every meeting in the country and in London to co-ordinate activity to support and 'was carried to the House wrapped in Flannels to vote for the repeal of that odious and detestable tax'.

> Our strong beer is taxed and we're taxed in our lights,
> And more would they tax of our natural rights
> But sooner than yield to a tax on our Fruit,
> Our trees though in blossom shall fall at the root.
>
> For this is the sound of the West Country Boys,
> Who Liberty prizes,
> Disdains and despises
> The thoughts and the threats of a general excise.

No domestic cause had ever so united the people of Somerset.

14
DRAGON OR WYVERN ?

IN recent decades the people of Somerset seem to have carried out an informal adoption. The object of all the attention has been a mythical beast – the wyvern. The Somerset County Council's social club is known as the Wyvern and the county town of Taunton also boasts a Wyvern Shopping Centre. Yeovil has Wyvern Boats Ltd., Seavington St Michael is the base for Wyvern Farm Services, Minehead delights in the Wyvern Travel Service, Wyverns of Bridgwater sell motor-cycles, Wyverns of Weston retail cars at Weston-super-Mare and there are many more examples which could be cited.

The Wyvern derives from the Saxon word for viper and was supposed to be a winged serpent. Heraldically it is depicted with two forelegs, wings and sitting on its curled barbed tail. The snag is that the Wyvern is *not* the emblem of Somerset, that honour falling to the four-legged dragon, a word which comes from the Greek for serpent, draco. The fact received official recognition on 29 December 1911 when Somerset County Council was granted its coat of arms, paid for by William Broadmead, depicting a red dragon rampant holding in its forelegs an upright blue mace, all on a gold background.

Existing accounts suggest that the dragon as used as a standard originated in the east, whence it was introduced to Europe by the Romans. In red or purple colouring it was borne both in war and on ceremonial occasions and early writers speak of it as a real creature rather than a fabulous beast. In England dragons were claimed to have been seen in the sky to herald Danish raids. A group of canons from Laon, visiting England in 1113, were recorded to have seen a dragon with five heads and fiery breadth destroying Christchurch in Hampshire, and a similar attack on shepherds and their flocks at Sudbury was supposedly witnessed in 1405.

Nearer to home, dragons form an essential part of the folklore of West Somerset. St Carantoc was said to have tamed a dragon which had menaced King Arthur's people around Carhampton, while a dragon that allegedly crept from the Quantocks and menaced the area as far

(Left): *The heraldic wyvern, erect, and* (Right) *The coat of arms of Somerset County Council, granted in 1911.*

as Williton was finally slain at Norton Fitzwarren. A third dragon or 'worm', as the English formerly called a dragon, was supposedly slain by a worthy knight at Trull. There are commentators who see in these dragon stories folk memories and fears of invading armies, either Roman or Saxon, who fought under dragon banners. Indeed one 18th century account even attributes the Norton dragon to one which grew out of the corruption of British dead slain at Norton camp by the Roman general, Ostorius. The Saxons were fighting under dragon standards by 752 when Cuthred, King of the West Saxons, confronted the Mercians at Burford. Such a banner is mentioned in accounts of the battle of Assandun between Edmund Ironside and the Danes in 1016, and another is clearly depicted on Harold's standard on the Bayeux tapestry. The dragon also figures largely in Welsh mythology, although probably not adopted as the national emblem of Wales until the beginning of the 15th century. The dragon ensign was popular with the Norman dukes, and Richard I used it as a battle standard on the First Crusade.

The cartographer John Speed in 1610 depicted the supposed arms of the West Saxons as a gold dragon rampant on a red background: I say supposed, because of course the art and practice of heraldry did not begin in England until the 12th century. When Somerset County Council received its 1911 grant of arms these colours were reversed and the mace added.

So much for dragons: but why has Somerset so warmly espoused the wyvern ? The answer seems to be that until the early 15th century English heraldry only knew of the two-legged dragon and that it was from that time onwards that the four-legged variety gradually became more popular. So perhaps the wyvern is not such an inappropriate image for Somerset after all.

15
A ROYAL BY-BLOW?

MANY kings of England have left illegitimate issue, both acknow-ledged or otherwise. The best-known in our part of the country was without question the Duke of Monmouth, son of Charles II and Lucy Walters. The most recent monarch to admit to children born on the wrong side of the blanket was William IV who left four such sons (including the first earl of Munster) and five daughters. Of similar issue by Edward VII, whose extra-marital activities are well-known and ex-tremely well-documented, nothing is known. Yet it seems unlikely that, given the kind of life that he led as Prince of Wales, there should have been no such children produced. Indeed, it now seems possible that at least one may have slipped through the net.

On 8 September 1915, not long after the outbreak of the First World War, there appeared this advertisement on the front page of *The Times*.

IF THE NURSE OR OTHER PERSONS WHO CAN GIVE PARTICULARS OF THE BIRTH OR PARENTAGE OF A MALE CHILD KNOWN BY REPUTE AS BERTIE (OR HERBERT) THOMAS, BORN IN OR ABOUT 1885, SOMEWHERE IN LONDON, SUCH CHILD BEING IN THE SAME YEAR PLACED IN THE CUSTODY OF ONE MARY STEER, A WASHERWOMAN, OF WITHYPOOL, SOMERSET, AND AFTERWARDS APPRENTICED TO A FARMER AT WITHYPOOL, SOMERSET, WILL COMMUNICATE WITH D.O. THOMAS, SOLICITOR, 21, YORK-STREET, SWANSEA, SHE OR THEY WILL BE SUITABLY REWARDED.

The advertisement from The Times, 1915, *which started an enquiry still unresolved over seventy years later.*

Bertie Thomas had moved to South Wales and, at the age of 30, tried to 'do his bit' and enlist in the Motor Transport Corps. The authorities requested his birth certificate and he, thinking that he had been born on Exmoor, applied to the Superintendent Registrar at Dulverton but without success. Similarly no record of the birth was located at the General Register Office in London. At Withypool he and his Swansea solicitor learned that Bertie had been born in July 1885, brought as an infant by train from London to Dulverton with a trained nurse and thence, at midnight, by carriage and pair to Withypool. On arrival there, as stated in the advertisement, the child was placed in the charge of washerwoman Mary Steer.

Mary Steer had been born at Knowstone, Devon, in 1820 as Mary Troud, and was married firstly to a Mr Crocker and secondly in 1879 at Dulverton Registry Office to a widowed blacksmith, John Steer. Steer died in 1895 and Mary, taken into Dulverton Union Workhouse early in 1903, died there on 31 January 1904. A seach of the 1891 Census Returns confirmed that Bertie Thomas, then aged 4 and living with Mary Steer at Mill Cleeve Cottage, Withypool, had been born in London.

There were stories of a substantial sum having been left for young Bertie Thomas's upbringing but, when old enough, he was apprenticed to local farmer John Williams and later found employment with him at Stone Farm, Exford. Williams was farming a mere 84 acres at Withypool in 1881 but by 1910 had amassed over 700 acres, although admittedly as tenant of Sir Charles Thomas Dyke Acland, Bart. The locals attributed this rise in Williams's fortunes to the arrival of the young boy. Bertie Thomas left Somerset for Wales shortly after the death of Mary Steer, the nearest person to a mother that he had ever known.

On his return to Withypool, Bertie Thomas heard from the local vicar, probably the Rev. Mr Newman, who then held the benefices of Withypool and Hawkridge, that the minister had thought it prudent to destroy certain papers left with him relating to the boy. He learned little more from the trained nurse, named Storey, who had accompanied the baby on the midnight journey and later died at Dulverton.

These then were the meagre facts behind the advertisement inserted in *The Times* in 1915. It elicited no response from those who might have known the truth although the story was taken up by the *South Wales Post*. When interviewed by that paper's reporter the Swansea solicitor was distressingly vague about the identity of those he believed to be the parents. He commented frustratingly, 'if my information is correct – and I have no reason to doubt it – then the young man comes from very high parentage indeed'.

That was as far as Bertie Thomas ever got in his search for the truth. Any papers amassed by the Swansea solicitor appear to have been lost and, although the quest was subsequently taken up by Bertie's son, Wilfred J.H. Thomas, who now lives at Wiveliscombe, no further revealing facts have come to light. The story has been re-run by the *West Somerset Free Press* on several occasions between 1957 and 1982 but no informant has yet come forward to solve the mystery.

It is possible that young Bertie was the result of an indiscretion by a member of the Acland family who owned so much of the land around Exford and Withypool and still flourish in Devon to this day. Their standing, however, was probably not sufficiently exalted to merit the description of 'very high parentage indeed'. Maybe the Aclands just over a century ago performed a very convenient service for a much more highly placed individual by accommodating young Bertie on an isolated part of their far-flung estates. Bertie Thomas himself seems to have had no doubts, for before he died he indicated to his own son, Wilfred, that their ancestor was a much more celebrated 'Bertie' – the future King of England.

16
UNBROKEN LINKS

S OMERSET is blessed with numerous examples of old estates which have passed from generation to generation through families that still flourish today. At a time when many of us change our houses once a decade and gad about the country in search of promotion, it may seem surprising that there are still those who have chosen to surround themselves with the same scenery century after century. They might in turn answer, 'yes, but what scenery !' True, many have had to sell off substantial areas of the property laboriously gathered by their ancestors, but there remain several who continue to dwell on the estates which their forebears have cultivated for centuries. These seem to be mainly concentrated in a relatively small region in the west of the county.

Crowcombe, which nestles at the western foot of the Quantock Hills, appears to have been held before his death in about 1130 by Wimond de Crowcombe. Some four generations later Godfrey de Crowcombe granted half the manor for the good of his soul to Studley Priory in Oxfordshire and this half became known as the manor of Crowcombe Studley from its owners. Godfrey established a weekly market and an annual fair in 1227 and also founded a borough at Crowcombe: a money-making venture which met with a signal lack of success. Crowcombe was not destined to become a second Birmingham or a Manchester and perhaps we should be grateful for that. There followed three successive lords named Simon de Crowcombe and after the death of the last c.1322 the remaining half of the manor passed to his niece who married John Biccombe.

The Biccombes had no coat of arms and they appropriated those of the de Crowcombes, depicting three crows, which the visitor to Crowcombe church can still see carved on two of the 16th century bench ends. After a further six generations Hugh Biccombe died in 1568, leaving two daughters, one of whom married Thomas Carew of Camerton and inherited Crowcombe Biccombe manor, thereafter known as Crowcombe Carew. Their descendant in the fifth generation, another Thomas, pulled

Crowcombe Court, c.1790, nestling below the Quantock Hills. It was built from 1724 by Thomas Parker and Nathaniel Ireson for Thomas Carew, MP. The earliest use of brick for a major Somerset house, it is now a nursing-home.

down the old manor-house, which had stood beside the church, and in the years following 1724 built the present Crowcombe Court, the earliest use of brick for a major house in Somerset.

On Thomas Carew's death in 1766 the manor passed to his daughter Elizabeth, wife of James Bernard, who died childless in 1805, and thence to her cousin, Mary Carew. She married a Shropshire gentleman, George Henry Warrington, who was persuaded to change his name to Carew. Their great-grandson died without issue in 1886 and his sister, Ethel, wife of Robert Cranmer Trollope, a distant relative of the novelist Anthony Trollope, became heir to the manor of Crowcombe Carew. In 1894 she bought the manor of Crowcombe Studley, in private hands since the dissolution of Studley Priory by Henry VIII in 1539, and thus reunited the old manor of Crowcombe, divided for over six centuries. Her grandson, Major T.F. Trollope-Bellew, sold Crowcombe Court but still lives at Crowcombe as lord of the manor by virtue of his direct descent from Wimond de Crowcombe in the early 12th century. Indeed the de Crowcombe family may well have been resident there from an even earlier date.

Another manor with a similar pedigree lies to the west of Crowcombe below the Brendon Hills. Nettlecombe, like Crowcombe, settled before the Norman Conquest and duly recorded in the Domesday Book, was granted c. 1160 by John Marshall to Hugh de Ralegh, Sheriff of Devon. Hugh, having no son, gave the manor to Warin son of his brother, Walter de Ralegh. Warin's son Wimond is claimed as the ancestor of a more famous Sir Walter Ralegh, born at a remote farmhouse in East Devon. Nettlecombe, however, was allotted to another son, Sir Warin, whose great-great-grandson, Sir John de Ralegh, fought at the battle of Crecy in 1346. One of Sir John's sons, Simon, was at Agincourt in 1415 and founded a chantry chapel on the south side of Nettlecombe church. One of his two sisters, Matilda, married Sir Thomas Chaucer, son of the poet, and the other, Joan, took a Cornish gentleman to the altar, John Whalesburgh of Whalesburgh. When Simon died childless in 1440 he left Nettlecombe to his nephew, Thomas Whalesburgh. Thomas, who died in 1481, was survived by an only daughter, Elizabeth, who married another Cornishman, John Trevelyan of Trevelyan in St Veep, near Fowey.

The Trevelyan family legend, dating at least from the 17th century, tells how their incredibly distant ancestor was the only survivor when the mythical land of Lyonesse sank beneath the waves, saved by his horse which bore him through the sea to the Cornish mainland. The family coat of arms and crest both illustrate the valiant steed. From John

An idyllic but over-idealised depiction of Nettlecombe Court and its adjoining parish church, c.1790.

Trevelyan, who died in 1492, there followed confusingly a further six successive John Trevelyans until George Trevelyan, who stoutly supported his king during the Civil War. Dying before the Restoration of Charles II, it was George's son, another George, who received a baronetcy in 1661 as a reward for his father's loyalty.

One of the second George's younger grandsons was ancestor of the branch of the family which settled at Wallington in Northumberland and sired the great historian, G.M. Trevelyan. The senior line continued at Nettlecombe into the present century but ended with the death of Sir Walter John Trevelyan in 1931. The family account is that Sir Walter's son and heir was caught indecently exposing himself on the steps of Bristol Public Library and the estates were left to the young man's sister Joan, wife of a prominent painter, Garnet Ruskin Wolseley. Her son, John Wolseley, who inherited his father's talent for painting and now lives mainly in Australia, is today lord of Nettlecombe manor as the descendant of those 12th century Raleghs, two of whose effigies still lie in the nearby parish church.

The manor-house, Nettlecombe Court, built by Sir John Trevelyan in the last years of the 16th century, has been leased to the Field Studies Council since 1965 as the Leonard Wills Field Centre for courses on ecology, art and local history. The Wolseleys have retreated to the late 18th century stable block which they share with a community of artists.

The family archives had been deposited at our Record Office long before I came to Somerset but I well recall an evening spent at Nettlecombe when I was sitting next to John Wolseley's young sons, William and Thomas, enjoying a late meal. I reached out to an adjacent bookshelf and took down a small wooden box which I opened to reveal, to the evident surprise of the family, some twenty medieval charters dating from the 13th century. Many still had their seals intact and on the backs of those same seals could still be seen the fingerprints of those who had impressed them centuries before: the direct ancestors of the two lads who sat beside me, wolfing their lemon fluff.

The hunt was then on as the boys and I ransacked the library for further archival treasures. A cardboard box was found containing apprenticeship indentures of the poor of Nettlecombe and a quantity of mouse droppings, the former having at some time strayed from the church chest, the latter clearly accumulated later ! Eventually there came to light the original 12th century charter by which John Marshall granted to Hugh de Ralegh his 'land of Netelcumba': the charter by which the Wolseleys still hold Nettlecombe manor over 800 years later. I cherish the memory of evenings such as that.

A little further to the north-west of Nettlecombe lies Dunster, complete with fairy-tale castle perched on a precipitous hill which commands magnificent views across the Bristol Channel to Wales. The castle itself dates from soon after the Norman Conquest and was originally the home of the Mohun family. In 1376 it was bought with its estates from Joan, Lady Mohun, by Elizabeth Luttrell for the then phenomenal sum of 5,000 marks or £3,334 in modern money, since the English mark was worth 13s. 4d. or ⅔ of £1. In fact the Luttrells bought only the reversion of the property because a life interest was retained by Lady Mohun. She clung grimly to life, outliving Elizabeth Luttrell, and died over a quarter of a century later.

Thus it was Elizabeth's son, Sir Hugh Luttrell, who finally took possession in 1404 and built the superb gatehouse which spans the path up

Dunster Castle, 1791. The building, bought by the Luttrell family in 1376, rises majestically above the silted-up estuary of the river Avill.

from the town below. Sir Hugh's grandson, Sir James Luttrell, backed the Lancastrians in the Wars of the Roses and died of his wounds after the second battle of St Albans in 1461. He was condemned retrospectively for high treason by the victorious Yorkists and his estates were granted to Sir William Herbert, later earl of Pembroke. After the final triumph of the house of York at the battle of Bosworth in 1485 Henry VII restored the family's estates to Sir James's son, another Sir Hugh.

Four generations later Thomas Luttrell was holding the castle for Parliament in the Civil War, although persuaded to surrender it to the Royalists in 1643, a year before his death. The young Prince of Wales, the future Charles II, stayed there for a time in 1645, shortly before Robert Blake forced a further surrender, but on that occasion to the Roundhead forces. Thomas's great-grandson, Alexander Luttrell, died in 1737, leaving an only daughter Margaret, with whom the male line of the Luttrells came to an end at Dunster. Margaret married her cousin, Henry Fownes, who subsequently took the surname of Luttrell in addition to his own.

It was Henry's great-grandson, George Fownes Luttrell, who in 1867 commissioned Anthony Salvin to convert the 16th century mansion, created by an earlier George, into the many-towered romantic castle which the public tours today. I recall going there to take part in a dramatic pageant, telling the story of St John's Ambulance from the crusades onwards, in the days when Mrs Alys Luttrell, the widow of GFL's grandson, was still in residence at the castle. According to the script I played a wounded 'night', clad from head to foot in string chainmail into which I crawled in the old billiard room which doubled as a changing room. Awaiting my 'entrance' in the little courtyard to the right of the main entrance, I had my ardour somewhat dampened when the adjacent shire horse, bearing a rider dressed as a medieval Luttrell, completely flooded the confined area !

Following Mrs Luttrell's death, her son, Lt-Col Walter Luttrell, presented Dunster Castle to the National Trust in 1976, exactly 600 years after his ancestress had purchased it. You, gentle reader, may suppose that six centuries of continuous ownership at Dunster does not compare with the eight centuries I have described at Crowcombe and Nettlecombe; but wait. Having bade farewell to Dunster Castle, Lt-Col Luttrell, Somerset's Lord Lieutenant, went home to the Court House at East Quantoxhead, set at the head of the Quantock Hills on the Bristol Channel coast.

The grouping at East Quantoxhead of manor-house, church, thatched

Cottages in East Quantoxhead village: owned by the Luttrells and their ancestors since before the Domesday Book was compiled in 1086.

cottages and millpond, complete with artistically placed ducks, must rank as one of the most appealing anywhere in England. Before the Norman Conquest the manor was owned by Merlesuain, a Saxon, but after Hastings it was granted to a Norman, Ralph Pagnell, as recorded in the Domesday Book of 1086. Ralph's granddaughter, Frethesant Pagnell, married a certain Geoffrey Luttrell: their son, Andrew Luttrell, inherited East Quantoxhead in 1232 and his descendants have held it ever since, although in continuous occupation only since 1888. Lt-Col Luttrell thus lives in a house which stands on land owned by his ancestor over 900 years ago.

I found it particularly piquant when in 1985 I addressed the English Speaking Union in Philadelphia on the subject of Somerset and projected a slide of Dunster Castle, my audience included an American Luttrell sitting in the front row. It is Australia, however, which today is probably graced with the presence of more Luttrells than either England or America, and in the direct male line too. Sir Andrew Luttrell of Dunster, who died in 1538, had a younger son, Nicholas, who moved to Honibere in Devon and from whom were descended the Luttrells of Saunton Court at Braunton in North Devon. Edward Luttrell, sixth in descent from Nicholas, was shot dead in a London scuffle in 1721 by two bailiffs who were trying to arrest him for debt. His son, Southcott Hungerford Luttrell, succeeded to the Saunton Court estate on the death of his cousin as a childless lunatic in 1751, but sold his inheritance only six years later. Two generations later another Edward Luttrell shook the dust of England off his feet and emigrated to Australia to spread the name of Luttrell on the other side of the globe. In recent years several of his descendants have contacted our Record Office to establish their Somerset links in time to celebrate the 1988 Bicentennial of their native land: an Antipodean sequel to a story that started in Somerset over nine centuries before.

17
THE CLERK OF THE WEATHER

To those searching out their family trees, as more and more 'ancestor worshippers' are doing these days, the registers of baptisms, marriages and burials kept in each individual parish provide a vital source. These registers are, however, usually rather boring documents, giving little or no indication of the personalities they record. Fortunately there are always exceptions.

Near Crewkerne lies the little village of Pendomer where between 1724 and 1768 the Rev James Upton served as rector. His father, of the same name, had been the most successful headmaster of Taunton Grammar School. The son, using several blank pages in the Pendomer register, made his own bid for immortality by entering details of improvements he had made in the parish, the weather and special events. He records that he rebuilt the rectory barn in 1729, retiled the parsonage and put up new rafters, 'the old ones being much rotted and decayed'. He predicted that 'the Great Comet of 1682', Halley's Comet, would appear again about 1757, and was only one year out. He was concerned that the National Debt had hit £47,373,532 in 1733 and horrified when it rose to £48,128,149 in the following year.

Upton judged the summer of 1735 to be the coldest and wettest 'that ever was known in the memory of man: no hot weather 'till the 29th of July', while the winters of 1749 and 1750 were 'the warmest and pleasantest that the oldest man I have met with ever rememberd', although the great rains in July 1751 meant an 'abundance of hay quite spoil'd'. And then, totally out of the blue at the foot of the page, without any indication of what led to the admission, Upton penned the revealing statement: 'He that followeth Truth too closely, may happen to get a Kick in the Chops' !

Over at Ubley on the Mendips in 1696, some time before James Upton ever arrived at Pendomer, the parish clerk, Edmund Dirrick, began a new parish register, bought from a Bristol stationer, Richard Gravett. Dirrick clearly fancied his own literary talents. When John Dirrick, 'a mindips man' (i.e. a lead miner) and probably Edmund's uncle, was buried

Anno 1722 I planted ye Orchard with Apple Trees which before was gone to ruin & decay.

Anno 1729 I built ye Barn new from ye ground & ye Room over

1733 I new tiled all ye House, & put up all new Rafters ye old ones being much rotted & decayed

Jacobus Upton A.M. Coll Wadhamensis Socius 1725

An° 1735 Higher Woodclose was cut to Beat 1735

The National Debt

| 1733 | 47,373,532 |
| 1734 | 48,128,149 |

The Great Comet of 1632 will appear again about 1757

1732 An excessive dry Summer.

1735 The coldest & Wettest Summer yt ever was known
ye same in ye memory of Man: No Hot weather till ye 29 of July
1751 August 2 Sam. Goodford Gen: obiit. 6 Septr.

In ye month of May 1738 I new thatch'd all ye West-end of ye house, & put up new Rafters, all ye old ones being rotten: & one new oaken Beam. J. Upton. New coated 1757

The Rev James Upton's jottings in Pendomer parish register.

in January 1705, the parish clerk broke into verse to give us a truly touching summation of the life of a Mendip miner.

> His constant Imployment was under ground,
>   His long distemper was shortnes of breath,
> His maine Indeavor was safe and sound.
>   He sett his affections above the earth,
> And after sixty and two years spent
>   In labour and sorrow, in grife and paine,
> Finding in earth no true content,
>   Surrendred his soul to god againe.

But it is with his descriptions of the extremes of Somerset weather that Edmund Dirrick really comes into his own. I can do no better than let him speak for himself, although I have modernized his spelling so that nothing stands between the man and his reader. For his first account he looked back some 13 years.

In the year 1683 was a mighty great frost. The like was not seen in England for many ages. It came upon a very deep snow which fell immediately after Christmas, and it continued until a Lady day [25 March]. The ground was not open, nor the snow clean gone off the earth in thirteen weeks; some of the snows remained at Mendip till Midsummer. It was so deep and driven with the wind against the hedges and stiles, that the next morning after it fell men could not go to their grounds to serve their cattle without great danger of being buried, for it was above head and shoulders in many places. Some it did bury and did betoken the burying of many more, which came to pass before the end of the year. But in a few days the frost came so fierce that people did go upon the top of it, over walls and stiles as on level ground, not seeing hardly where they was, and many men was forced to keep their cattle until the last in the same ground that they was in at first, because they could not drive them to any other place, and did hew the ice every day for water. By reason of the sharpness of the frost and the deepness of the snow, some that was travelling on Mendip did travel till they could travel no longer and then lie down and die. But mortality did prevail most among them that could travel worst. The sharpness of the season took off the most part of them that was under infirmities. The people did die so fast that it was the greatest part of their work (which was appointed to do that work) to bury the dead; it being a day's work for two men, or two days' work for one man, to make a grave. It was almost as hard a work to hew a grave out in the earth as in the rock. The frost was a foot and half and two foot deep in the dry earth and, where there was moisture and water did run, the ice was a yard and four foot thick, insomuch that the people did keep market on the river. God doth scatter his ice like morsels, man cannot abide his cold: Psalm 147.17.

Nationally most of the forest trees split with the frost, the ice was 11 ins thick on the Thames and most of the birds died.

He then went on to describe the 'terible tempest both of watter and wind' that struck on 26 November 1703.

It began on Friday with rain, which caused a great flood before it ceased. Towards the evening the rain abated and the wind arised and so continued, rising higher and higher until about midnight, at which time it was so high the like was never known. The noise of it was like continual thunder, which did awaken all of us out of sleep. And feeling our beds shake under us and hearing our houses creak over us, none that was able to rise could lie on their beds. About four hours before day our houses began to break and in one hour's time a sad distraction there was. But none could go forth of their houses nor rise from their places to see what hurt was done because of the darkness and the danger for four or five hours, but sat, mourning, one with another and wishing for the day. But when the day was come, that we could look forth, lo, a woeful sight to behold. To see heaps of healm at our doors, the streets filled with thatch and tile of our houses: to see some houses blown down, many uncovered, and all in general torn and broken, more or less. To see the churches defaced, the towers was shaken, the windows broken, the lead blown off and the battlements thrown down. To see abundance of trees, especially elms, lying in the ways and in the fields with their roots turned upwards: a multitude of apple trees and many whole orchards wholly laid down. To see the corn mows uncovered and blown about the bartons, the hay mows thrown down and carried into the ditches. A woeful sight, indeed: enough to make anyone fear and tremble. To see everything that was not blown down, the hedges and trees and everything moveable, to quiver and shake. To see nothing but ruin and destruction on every side. If you look to the north, it was all laid down before you: if to the south, it was all coming towards you. If you look to the east, all was flying from you: if to the west it was all ready to fall upon you; with a great roaring over your heads and round about you. Thus it was with us, but with many more much worse. At the same time there was a very great loss at sea, both of ships and of men, and also in seaport towns in houses and in goods. The wind continuing hard on Saturday morning, it caused the sea to come in with such great force and strength, that on a sudden it filled all the channels, threw down the walls and broke down the banks, so that it overspread very much dry land; whereby those that inhabited on the borders thereof, having received as much hurt by the wind as others had, they received much more by the water. Their ground was spoiled, their cattle was drowned, their corn and hay was carried away and the greatest part of it was lost. Their gates was unhinged, their doors broke open, their goods swimmed in their houses and they themselves was in great danger, their houses being full of water at the bottom and blown off at the top. Some of them which was within was fain to stand on the walls of

A true report of certaine wonderfull ouerflowings
of Waters, now lately in Summerset-shire, Norfolke, and other
places of England: destroying many thousands of men, women,
and children, ouerthrowing and bearing downe
whole townes and villages, and drowning
infinite numbers of sheepe and
other Cattle.

A graphic portrayal of another 17th century flood in Somerset.

their houses, others, which was without, on the tops of trees to save their lives. Some of them remained so part of two days. Some went on foot in water to the girdle: others rode a horseback in water to the saddle, carrying their children at their backs to keep them alive. Some lost their lives. Many escaped very hardly and it was the Lord's mercy we had not been all consumed but, God being merciful unto us, we are almost all of us preserved. To him therefore be all glory, praise and thanksgiving, both now and for evermore. Amen.

This was the storm that swept away the Eddystone lighthouse, sank most of the Royal Navy and killed Richard Kidder, the Bishop of Bath and Wells, and his wife in bed at the Bishop's Palace at Wells. Six years later Edmund Dirrick took up his pen again.

The year 1709 was almost like to a famine: not for want of rain, but clean contrary. For, next to our sins, it was the abundance of rain that was the cause of it. By reason of much rain, there was but little or no good hay made in the summer. The dumb cattle for our sakes suffered in the winter. The oxen was so weak that they could hardly work. The cows did miscarry and many of them perish in calving: the sheep was banned almost all in general. The very hares did lie dead in the hedges. The corn was great part washed away by reason of much rain, and the rest withered by reason of long wet. That of it which did remain till harvest was half spoiled before it could be cut and carried. Wheat was sold for 10s the bushel, barley for 5s and 6d, malt for 6s, beans for 5s, peas for 6s. Wheat bread was at 4d a pound, cream cheese at the same price, beef at 3½d, bacon at 7d. Sufficient people and good housekeepers did bake barley and beans and did eat no other bread. Labouring men and poor people did boil beans and water, and did eat it without bread. If a poor woman could make a hard shift to get a peck of malt to make small drink, she had as hard a work to get barm [yeast] to ripen it because there was so much barley baked and so little best drink brewed. Barm was sold for 12d a pint. It was a very hard matter for a poor man to come by a pound of good bread or a pint of good drink. And thus it continued until the end of the year, or rather worse; for, when the season came to put seed into the ground for another year, it did so shrink the store that what was dear before could hardly be got for money. Boiling peas was at 2s the peck, barley at 6s the bushel. The generality of ordinary people did so much rely upon beans and barley, till it was much dearer after the rate than wheat. For, when it pleased God to send dry weather and corn being likely to be good on the ground, wheat fell to 7s and 6s and 6d the bushel; so that in a few months we could say with the Psalmist that the valleys were so covered with corn that men did rejoice and sing: Psalms 65.13. Yet all this while the Lord did provide for us and preserved us. There was still something to fill the mouth, though many times the belly was not well filled. That saying is true: He that sendeth mouths sendeth meat.

Dirrick even indicated the motives which lay behind his meteorological chronicle.

This may be written for the generation to come, that they may hear and fear; that they may hear what God hath done and fear Him who only can do such great things. But I fear it will be too soon forgotten, when the smart of it is a little over: especially in the next age, when all the eye witnesses are dead and all the suffering members are taken away. Then it will be counted strange things (as indeed it is), and perhaps with some more stranger than true.

Edmund Dirrick was buried at Ubley on 29 November 1713 but his vivid descriptions live on, to conjure up the often harsh life led by the people of one Mendip village some three centuries ago.

18

CUDGEL PLAYING

IN 1979 the South Somerset Agricultural Preservation Society, something of a mouthful, planned to revive what was once one of
Somerset's most popular sports – cudgel playing. In Somerset the
pastime was known in its various forms as backsword, sword and dagger,
butts and cudgels and singlestick. In origin it seems to have been the
poor man's equivalent of fencing, derived from the medieval use of the
quarterstaff but with a much shorter stick. Indeed backsword play using a
wooden weapon was practised in the Royal Navy to train recruits to
wield a cutlass.

The object of the contest was to 'break' your opponent's head and
'save' your own. In Somerset a bout usually ended when blood ran from
the head to within an inch of the eyebrow: although some matches
were concluded if any blood was seen to flow above the neck. Certain
gamesters even 'drank gunpowder' before a contest in the belief that this
inhibited the flow of blood.

In backsword or singlestick each man had his left hand tied behind his
back or, with a handkerchief or strap, to the front of his left thigh. The art
lay in tying the left hand sufficiently loosely to enable the elbow to be
raised to protect the left side of the head. In defence the cudgel was held
at an angle in front of the face: in attack, if the head was too securely
defended, the assailant would beat his opposite number about the legs.

The stick used was generally an ash plant between three and four feet
long with a large wickerwork basket handle resembling that of a cutlass.
During the fight this protected the knuckles, was raised to receive the
heavier blows and could be used afterwards to collect money from the
spectators. This basket was commonly known in Somerset as the 'butt'
and elsewhere as the 'pet'. Sometimes the butt was merely an improvised
cloth padding or a garment wrapped around the arm.

Each contestant was attended by three seconds or 'sticklers' and
before each bout the men shook hands and muttered the time-honoured
formula 'keep up your butt and God preserve your eyesight'. This was
no meaningless ritual for in the 1890s one old Somerset backsword

Single-stick playing outside a village inn.

player recalled having seen 'a man's eye cut clean out of his head by a blow'. The participants stood about three feet apart or even closer and enthusiastically belaboured each other until one cried 'hold' or the required amount of blood was shed. If 'hold' was called there was a break of one minute before the battle was rejoined. In butts and cudgels or sword and dagger two sticks were used: a short one with a protected handle for defence and a longer one for attack.

Contests at fairs and revels were clearly common in both the 16th and 17th centuries but reached their greatest popularity in the second half of the 18th century. Usually organized by the landlord of an inn to increase his takings, matches lasted between one and three days, prizes being subscribed for in advance by the potential spectators – usually the gentry of the neighbourhood. The competitors also had to apply in advance so that they could be 'ticketed': evidently a form of draw to decide how the gamesters should be matched. Surviving accounts indicate that an unfenced stage was set up on which the fights took place, usually formed by placing planks across beer barrels.

On occasions the gamesters were used to provide political muscle. In 1688 cudgel players from Wellington and North Petherton were brought into Taunton by the Tories to beat up Whig electors when they tried to

This is to give NOTICE,

THAT on *Wednesday* and *Thursday* the 14th and 15th of *September* next, will be play'd for at SWORD and DAGGER, at the GEORGE INN in *Martock, Somerset*, Two Silver Bowls, valued at Three Pounds, free, only paying Half a Crown to the House each Bowl.

☞ Good Encouragement will be given by the Gentlemen.

TO be play'd for at SWORD and DAGGER, on Monday the 3d and Tuesday the 4th Days of September next, in High Street, in Taunton, in the County of Somerset, between the Sarazen's-Head and the George Inns there, the Sum of Two Guineas and Half at least each Day, *viz.* Two Guineas to the best Gamester, and Half a Guinea to the Second Best; when fair Shirts will be provided for the Players.

N. B. There will be a good Ordinary for the Gentlemen one Day at the George, and the other Day at the Sarazen's-Head.

☞ The Gamesters to mount the Stage each Day at Ten o'Clock.

THERE will be played for the Second and Third of September, at Sword and Dagger, at the Red-Lyon in Hatchbeauchamp, a Purse of Guineas, where all Gamesters, are desired to meet, and enter their Names, and draw Tickets. It is Six Miles from Chard, five from Ilminster, and five from Taunton.

Eight Guineas

TO be play'd for at Butts and Cudgels, on Monday and Tuesday the 15th and 16th of June next, at the Castle in Taunton. —— The Conditions are as follow:—Two guineas to be play'd for on the Monday in the forenoon, and two guineas in the afternoon: Two guineas on the Tuesday morning, and two guineas in the afternoon. The gamesters to mount ready dress at ten o'clock each morning, and each party is expected to bring proper dressers. The whole a free gift.

N. B. It is imagined that Dorsetshire gamesters will play against the west.

Advertisement for cudgel matches at Martock, 1748, Taunton, 1750, Hatch Beauchamp, 1760, and Taunton Castle, 1772.

vote. Contests staged in Taunton included a sword and dagger match at the West Country House Inn for two silver bowls on successive days in July 1744 and the prize of a hat for backsword on the third day. In 1750 the landlords of the Saracen's Head and George Inn, both in Taunton's High Street, jointly staged a two-day sword and dagger match, the inns taking turns to provide a profitable 'ordinary' or meal for the onlookers. In 1751 a butt and cudgel match was held at the Half Moon Inn, in 1761 and 1771 at the Three Cups (now the County Hotel), and in 1772 at Taunton Castle, when the Dorset gamesters challenged the West of England.

Taunton had no monopoly in the sport. Parson James Woodforde attended cudgel battles at Castle Cary in 1769 and 1771, staged on the anniversaries of George III's coronation, and contributed 4s 5d. to the purse on one occasion. In an age when the other popular sport was cockfighting, the bloodthirsty nature of the exhibitions was openly accepted. One Somerset clergyman recalled in his boyhood days at Wells in the early 19th century how the Bishop of Bath and Wells was an avid spectator. The men of Somerset had boundless confidence in their prowess and in 1780 at the Golden Lion, Wrington, and at the Bradford Inn, Bradford-on-Tone, challenged 'the Rest of the World' to meet them at backsword and sword and dagger. Just in case the rest of the world failed to rise to the bait they arranged to match against each other. Further competitions are recorded at Tintinhull, Yeovil and, in 1771, at Crewkerne, when the gamesters fought continuously for seven hours at the George Inn.

After the close of the 18th century the sport's popularity declined. It was revived briefly at the Black Horse Inn, North Town, Taunton, in June 1830 when players from Wiveliscombe met others from Long Load and Burrowbridge. One of the last recorded meetings in the Taunton area was staged on 25 July 1836 at the Lethbridge Arms, Bishops Lydeard, the men of Wiveliscombe being again in evidence. Elsewhere lesser contests continued at village revels and fairs, particularly at Wedmore where several families became legendary for the cudgel players they produced in successive generations. In 1857 John Bunn of Wedmore was proclaimed backsword champion at the celebrations to mark the periodic scouring of the Uffington White Horse in Berkshire. The final decline in Somerset is dated by F.T. Elworthy to the period 1860-70.

It will come as no surprise to learn that the efforts made in 1979 to revive this little-remembered and barbaric blood sport met with a signal lack of success.

19

THE BURNING OF WOMEN

IT may seem amazing today, but until two hundred years ago we were still legally executing women by burning them alive in public. This dreadful sentence was imposed when women were convicted of the offence of Petty Treason. The crime first appeared on the Statute books in 1352 under an Act of Edward III and was committed when 'a servant slayeth his master, or a wife her husband, or when a man, secular or religious, slayeth his prelate, to whom he oweth faith and obedience'. Petty Treason, like High Treason, was seen as an action against established authority and, as such, had to be crushed by the courts.

The penalty for Petty Treason was identical to that imposed for High Treason, namely that the criminal was to be hanged, drawn and quartered. In cases involving women it was considered unseemly for their bodies to be exposed and publicly hacked into four pieces by the executioner and thus burning was substituted as a more appropriate alternative. Blackstone, one of England's most celebrated legal commentators, considered that this form of execution had been handed down from the Druids, who were also believed to have burned women for murdering their husbands.

One particularly unpleasant case involved Susannah Davis of Chilton Trinity near Bridgwater who was married on 5 March 1753 at Durleigh to John Bruford of West Monkton, just to the east of Taunton. Only two months after her wedding she decided to murder her husband, having taken another lover. She added arsenic to his ale 'but he, perceiving it gritty, drank but little'. Thereupon she mixed sufficient to kill twenty men with flour of brimstone, a medicine that her husband was taking, and he lingered for four days before dying in agony. She was only nineteen.

The sequel was played out at Cure Green near Wells on 3 September, as described for its readers by the *Western Flying Post*. 'She was drawn to the place of execution on a sledge, dressed in a black gown with a black hood over her head. When she was brought to the stake she prayed with the clergyman that attended her above half an hour and behaved very

The barbaric burning of a woman for the murder of her husband in 18th century England.

decent and becoming. She was then set on a stool or trippet and when the rope was put about her neck she pray'd and said "O Lord forgive me and receive my soul !" And standing two or three minutes she dropped a black handkerchief, which she had in her hand, as a signal and was then turned off. The faggots were then placed round her and a barrel of pitch set under them. Two plates of iron were put round her body and nailed to the stake to keep her up while she was consuming. In about ten minutes after she was turned off the faggots were set on fire and burnt for about an hour with great fury, by which time she was almost consumed. A small coffin was prepar'd to put those few remains of her that were left into, in order to be buried. She acknowledged the crime for which she suffered, was willing to die for it, and forgave all the world, as she hoped to be forgiven. There was a prodigious concourse of spectators to see the execution." The Durleigh parish register, recording the wedding, added 'an unfortunate marriage ! She poison'd him and was burnt for so doing at Wells ye ensuing autumn.' 'Turned off' in the above account alludes to the executioner's practice of mercifully strangling the unfortunate women before the fire was lit.

The last such case so far noted in Somerset took place at Ilchester at 3.15 pm on 8 May 1765. Mary Norwood had been married to her husband when she was only 18 and he 45. After fifteen years of marriage she was seduced by an Axbridge shoemaker and poisoned her husband's breakfast milk. According to the same newspaper she 'was brought to the place of execution at Ivelchester covered with a pitch garment. She was first strangled and, after she was dead, the faggots were set on fire which, presently communicating with her pitch garment soon reduced her to ashes. She died penitent, calling on God for mercy and desiring all people to take warning by her shameful death. She obstinately denied the horrid deed until two days before her execution, in hopes of getting a longer reprieve; but being told by the Keeper she could not expect it and that she was to die on the above day, she confessed.'

This barbaric form of execution continued in force as late as 1790. It was a Somerset banker, Sir Benjamin Hammet, MP for Taunton, who in that year introduced a bill to outlaw the burning of women for High or Petty Treason and to substitute hanging, as in the case of all other murders, and thus brought to an end the tragic catalogue of vicious executions over the centuries.

Henry VII – royal visitor to Taunton in 1497.

20

A RIGHT ROYAL DAY

ON 8 May 1987, in almost unbroken sunshine, HM Queen Elizabeth and HRH the Duke of Edinburgh spent the day being feted by the towns of Taunton and Bridgwater. The first phase of a new hospital was opened, factories and recent developments inspected, in a demanding succession of engagements. The Queen has made innumerable such visits to cities, towns and villages throughout the United Kingdom but there was one fact which set that day apart from all others. The 8 May 1987 was arguably the first occasion on which an English monarch had made an official visit to Taunton for 490 years and to Bridgwater for 301 years.

There can be few if any English towns of comparable size, certainly I have never come across any, which have suffered from such avoidance over similar lengths of time. From the moment that I moved to Taunton twenty-three years ago I was regularly informed of the fact by the proverbial men and women in the street. There seemed to be an almost perverse sense of pride in those who recounted the tale and all, without exception, claimed that the neglect stemmed from the support which both towns had given to the Duke of Monmouth and his ill-fated attempt to capture the throne in 1685.

The folk-memory of the Monmouth episode, and the Bloody Assizes which followed it, is still strong in Somerset and has led to the perpetration of many historical fictions, a number of which are dealt with elsewhere in this volume. One account retailed to me by my good friend and fellow music-maker, Brian Cresswell, gave some credence to the local belief in a royal snub. An army acquaintance of his was apparently being inspected by a prominent member of the royal family who politely enquired where he came from. 'Bridgwater, Ma'am', was the reply, whereupon the royal nose was raised and the retort 'Sedgemoor country, eh ?' slipped from the royal lips.

Taunton's last visit from the sovereign was believed to have been in 1497 when Henry VII, following Perkin Warbeck's rebellion, spent a few days in the town and questioned the would-be usurper in person. The

Privy Purse accounts include the sum of £9 'for the Kinges losse at cardes at Tawnton', but surely this ill fortune could not explain why English monarchs gave the place such a wide berth for so long. One recent book on the Monmouth Rebellion, David Chandler's *Sedgemoor 1685* (1985), alleged that 'by August 1685 [sic – 1686] the situation had so far returned to normal that King James II was able to pay a visit to Bridgwater and Taunton in person'. That the king never reached Taunton is made clear in a hitherto unpublished document written by the Rev Andrew Paschall, rector of Chedzoy, which I discovered at the British Library.

This describes how James left Bristol on 27 August 1686 to visit the battlefield. 'After a full view taken of ye place, his Majesty rode to Bridgwater, where was presented an addresse from Taunton and an invitation to their town. But his Majesty was to dine next day at my Lord Fitz Harding's and lodge at Wilton [near Salisbury], 40 miles off, so he went away early next morn, pleased I heare with his reception at Bristoll, not so well with that at Bridgwater'. On a personal note Paschall added that he 'had ye honour of being remembred by his Majesty and of kissing his hand in Bridgwater'.

Bridgwater people had always told the story that Queen Victoria had ordered the blinds on the royal train to be pulled down as she steamed through that town. In 1978, in a letter to the Bridgwater MP, Tom King, Sir Robin Mackworth Young, the royal librarian, claimed that Victoria had never travelled to the West Country by train but only visited it in the royal yacht, an assertion which I was able to challenge in the columns of the *Bridgwater Mercury*. In 1856 the Queen, Prince Albert and their children had indeed sailed down the English Channel in the royal yacht and landed at Plymouth. With stormy weather in the channel, they decided on 15 August to return to their Isle of Wight home, Osborne House, by train, going by way of Exeter, Taunton, Bridgwater, Bristol and Salisbury.

According to the *Taunton Courier*, the Queen agreed to leave the train to meet local dignitaries only at Exeter, Bristol and Salisbury. The royal train had to stop for several minutes at Taunton to take on water but, although the borough's MP, Henry Labouchere, a personal friend of the royal family, tried to persuade Victoria to alight, she declined to do so. There is no reference to the train even slowing down as it passed through Bridgwater, as it did at Bath. It was August, quite likely to have been a sunny day and the blinds of the royal compartment may well have been drawn down on the Queen's order. Thus do popular stories

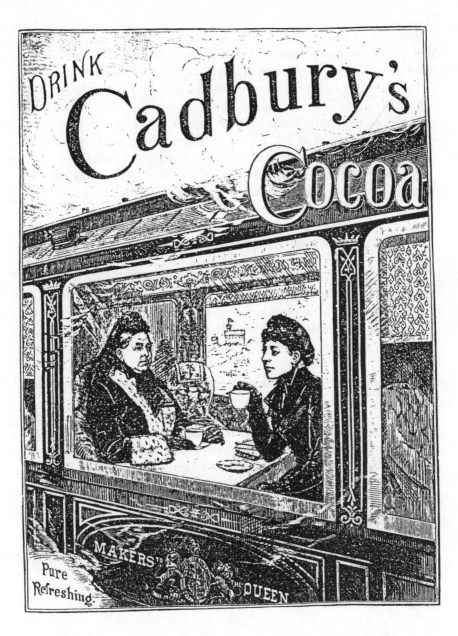

Queen Victoria travelling with the Princess Royal on the Great Western Railway: as she did when she passed through Taunton and Bridgwater in 1856.

have their beginnings.

It was in 1916 that Thomas Patton in his book of reminiscences, *Wise Men of the West*, first commented in print on the lack of 'any state visit to Taunton by a royal personage'. There had, however, been a few members of the royal family who had come to the town since 1685: William Henry, Duke of Gloucester, in 1766, the Prince of Wales, who stayed incognito at the Castle Hotel in 1856, and Alfred, Duke of Edinburgh, who was snowed up at Gill's Great Western Hotel for three days in 1891. It was only the monarch who had not been in evidence.

A further occasion which has led to a degree of debate was the visit of King George VI, soon after his Coronation, when he arrived at Taunton station to make a tour of the Duchy of Cornwall estates in December 1937. Having spent the night on the royal train which had been parked in a railway siding at Norton Fitzwarren, he was greeted on the platform at Taunton by the Mayor, inspected troops outside the station and then drove through and out of the town to Curry Mallet. Whether or not this lightning tour constituted an official visitation excited considerable correspondence in the local press in 1987.

I had first commented publicly on the lack of a visit by the sovereign in 1977, when my *Book of Taunton* was issued, and the point was taken up in newspapers which reviewed the work, notably in the *Guardian*. Thereafter the topic resurfaced periodically in the papers. I suspect that Buckingham Palace Press Office must have grown weary of denying that Taunton and Bridgwater were on a monarchical blacklist. Indeed, I doubt that in their heart of hearts the men of Somerset ever really believed that successive sovereigns on their death beds raised themselves painfully on one elbow and muttered 'son, never go to Taunton !'

The question, however, was raised privately on a number of occasions with individual members of the royal family and, eventually, by Lt-Col Walter Luttrell, Somerset's Lord Lieutenant, with Prince Philip. The Prince's reaction was reportedly explosive, incredulous and unprintable. According to Col Luttrell, it was this conversation which led directly to the Queen's sunkissed visit to both towns in 1987.

The story, which had run and run for nearly five centuries, had finally ended.

21

THE VIGOROUS VIGORS

I T is often fascinating how far back a name can be traced. In 1986 the
Somerset Record Office received a letter from the granddaughter of
Major Sir John St Vigor Fox (1879-1968) of Westholme House, Pilton,
near Shepton Mallet. She was concerned in tracing the origin of his
second Christian name. At that time she had successfully pursued the line
back to Sir John's great-grandfather, William Fox, a Manchester merchant, who had married Abigail daughter of Joseph Vigor, another merchant from Manchester. Her researches showed that Joseph was in turn
the son of Joseph Vigor of Bristol who had been born in 1654 and in
1679 married Abigail North.

That was as far as the lady had managed to track the ancestry but she
had found that the Bristol Joseph had held lands in Hemington, a parish
three miles east of Radstock in Somerset. From my point of view it was
the work of a moment to consult the Hemington parish registers, which
revealed that Joseph son of John and Hester Vigor of Folkland had
been baptised there on 6 August 1654. Folkland is to be identified with
Falkland, a hamlet lying 1¼ miles northeast from Hemington church.

Joseph Vigor's baptism at Hemington on 6 August 1654, linking the families of
Somerset and Bristol.

John and Hester Vigor were clearly of reasonable standing at Falkland as their servant, Margaret Howell, was buried at Hemington in 1641, and they had eight other children baptised there between 1642 and 1660. There were two possible baptisms for John Vigor – as a son of John Vigor of Hassage (also in Hemington) in 1613 or a son of William Vigor in 1608. As William had seven other children baptised between 1606 and 1619 at which ceremonies he was usually described as 'of Folkland', it was probably he who was the next ancestor. William son of John Vygor was christened at Hemington in 1576.

Before this time the Hemington parish registers do not enter the names of parents of those baptised and have gaps for the periods 1543-44, 1553-57 and 1563-68. Children named John Vygor were baptised in 1540, 1546 and 1549. Without protracted research, it did not appear possible to trace the family any further back with certainty. As for the name itself, however, the accepted authority, P.H. Reaney, in his *Dictionary of British Surnames*, considered that it derived from the Old French and indicated one displaying vigour or liveliness.

The researcher should never give up too soon. According to the Rev John Collinson's *History of Somerset* (1791), Nicholas de Sancto Vigore in the reign of Henry V (1413-1422) held one quarter of a knight's fee in Falkland. Falkland is such a tiny settlement and the surname sufficiently rare for it to be inconceivable that the later Vigor family was not descended from Nicholas. Again, it is not possible to discover Nicholas's ancestors generation by generation, but the surname occurs remarkably frequently in the same area of Somerset in the 13th century. Thus Thomas de Sancto Vigore (Sheriff of Somerset 1269-71, died 1295) and his son Thomas (born about 1259) held the manor of Stratton St Vigor, later Stratton on the Fosse, which the son sold to Thomas de Gurney in 1308. Similarly, Beatrix de Sancto Vigore, widow, granted lands at Stratton to Glastonbury Abbey in 1263 and William de Saint Vigor was one of the most powerful men in Somerset as abbot of Glastonbury 1219-23.

William had been elected abbot of Glastonbury on his return from a mission to Rome and proved, in his own abbey at least, a most popular choice. According to John of Glastonbury's history of the abbey , 'he set tyranny aside and with paternal concern fostered the monks as he would sons, freely conferring many gifts upon them for their bodies' recreation'. Among his many reforms, 'in order to improve the convent's beer, he added half again as much grain and oats to each brew' and 'increased three standard loaves by a quarter of a loaf, so that they equalled a conventual loaf'. Following his death on 18 September 1223, he was buried on the north side of the chapter house.

Possibly the historian should be satisfied at this point, but it is tempting to ask how the family got its name. They were clearly French, probably Norman, and presumably came to England in the later 11th or 12th century. There is a town near Bayeux called Saint-Vigeur-le-Grand, where a monastery was founded in the early 6th century by St Vigor himself, which may well have been the family's original home.

St Vigor was born at Artois, educated at Arras and became a preaching hermit at Raviere. Following his ordination as a priest, he continued his missionary activity on a grander scale. He was appointed bishop of Bayeux in 513 and was principally remembered for his opposition to idol-worship, destroying a particularly important idol and erecting a church in its place. He died in about 537 and shares his feast day, 1 November, with All Saints.

From a small Somerset hamlet in the mid 17th century it has proved possible to journey back through a succession of admittedly tenuous links to 6th century France. The study of names can indeed be an absorbing one.

22

V.C.H. SOM

THE title of this chapter usually appears only in a footnote and is the abbreviated way of referring to the *Victoria History of Somerset*. Of this great work five volumes have already seen the light of day and at least sixteen have still to be researched, written and published. The first two volumes, concerned with general subjects, appeared before the First World War as part of a grand but private design to cover the whole country. Almost inevitably the project proved too expensive to finance and none of the work on the histories of individual Somerset parishes appeared in print.

The grand scheme was restarted in 1967 under the joint patronage of the Somerset County Council and the University of London with the appointment of my former colleague, Dr Robert Dunning, as editor, and I joined him a year later. In eight years I completed the histories of twenty parishes, the largest of which, Crewkerne, was written together with Dr Dunning.

It was a fascinating period in my working life and, thanks largely to Robert Dunning, I learned a great deal about the practi- calities of historical research: the little details that do not appear on the syllabus for an Oxford University history degree. Most rewarding was the affection that I developed for the parishes which I researched: an almost proprietory feeling for each and every one of them, which remains with me to this day.

The first place on which I was let loose, East Lydford, lies adjacent to the Fosse Way, some five miles east of Somerton. It was a small parish, anciently 708 acres but reduced in 1884 to a mere 644 acres. The reduction in its area was achieved by transferring a detached 'island' of the parish called Fourfoot, lying two miles to the northeast. This area had formerly been known as Raynes or Reynolds Wood, evidently from the Reigny family who were lords of the manor in the 13th and 14th centuries, and it soon became clear that the 'island' of ground had been allotted to East Lydford to provide a source of timber. Beside the Fosse Way on this same 'island' stood a public house, later Fourfoot Farm,

The many-signed former inn: Fourfoot near East Lydford.

which adopted as many different innsigns in as short a time as any I have ever known. Betweeen 1732 and 1859, a little over a century, it was known variously as the Maiden Head, the Three Horseshoes, the White Swan, the Nut Tree, the Blue Boy, the Buffalo's Head and the Colston's Arms.

One lesson I learned the hard way while working on East Lydford arose from its church. The old parish church had stood down by the banks of the River Brue but the churchwardens' accounts show that it was regularly flooded and the churchyard walls periodically washed away. Fortunately the parish secured its personal saviour in the shape of the Rev J.J. Moss, who in 1866 completed a new church in memory of his dear departed wife on higher, drier ground. Its architecture might charitably be described as Gothic/Early English and would have gladdened the heart of the late Sir John Betjeman but precious few others.

I remember quite clearly on a delightfully sunny day driving down to East Lydford for the first time to inspect the church. I recall walking round the interior of the building, noting the items brought from the old church – the font, the pulpit, the benchends – and then my eye lighted on two rectangular blocks of stone set in the west wall. Even to my relatively untutored eye it was clear that these bore ancient classical inscriptions in Latin. I got pardonably excited because, as far as I knew, no one had ever noticed or commented on these before: not even Sir

Nikolas Pevsner in his *Buildings of England* series. I recall walking out through the porch into the brilliant sunshine and looking across a mere two fields to the Roman Fosse Way. Already a little scenario was unfolding in my mind. I could almost see two old men digging a nearby ditch, one of their spades striking something hard and him turning to his friend to exclaim 'Look 'ere, George, look what I've found'. Perhaps the rector was then passing and gave them sixpence for their finds and asked himself how he could preserve those two venerable monuments of antiquity. Maybe his new church was then rising and so he set them in the west wall for the benefit of posterity.

As soon as I got back to Taunton I rang up a fellow antiquarian, Leonard Hayward, one of the leading Yeovil lights in archaeology, and told him of my find. I suspect that even then each of us visualised a learned paper contributed to the *Proceedings of the Somerset Archaeological Society* entitled 'Two hitherto unknown Roman inscriptions discovered in the parish church of East Lydford' by Robin Bush and Leonard Hayward: or, if he was doing the thinking, by Leonard Hayward and Robin Bush.

Shortly after that I collected the East Lydford parish records to take them in for deposit at the Somerset Record Office. As part of my work on the parish I eventually worked through these documents and came across an old dogeared exercise book in the handwriting I had already come to recognize as that of the Rev J.J. Moss, the builder of the church. There I found a reference to a holiday he had taken: a holiday in – Rome. He had apparently gone down into the catacombs and tripped over these two Roman inscriptions and, in the finest traditions of the English clergy, had liberated them. I was almost able to visualize Moss staggering back across Europe, bowed down with their weight, all the way to East Lydford to install them in his new church. The entire exercise had clearly been devised by fate specifically to deceive a young, numb, dumb, green local historian who was due there in a hundred years time – ME !

I hope the experience taught me a lesson – possibly even a number of lessons. You see, there was no reason on this earth why, at some time during the last century, that old exercise book should not have been lost, burned or discarded. And if it had been, there would by now be a learned paper entitled 'Two hitherto unknown Roman inscriptions ....' So don't necessarily believe all that you read in print.

As with all research the real fun lay in solving problems. I recall, when working on the parish of Shepton Beauchamp, near Ilminster, trying to find where in the parish the medieval market and two fairs were held. All had been discontinued in the earlier 16th century and, although I had come across the placename 'Shambles', I had been unable to discover its location, which did not appear on any of the available maps. I happened to drop in on the village school and one young lad solved my problem in a matter of seconds by identifying the Shambles, and thus the former market place, as having been at the right-angle bend in the main street through the village near the Duke of York inn, even though it was well over four centuries since the market had finally closed.

There are several Somerset parishes whose residents recount, without any foundation, that they were the birthplace of Jane Seymour, fourth wife of Henry VIII. These stories clearly came into being because the much landed Seymours were lords of many manors, among them Shepton Beauchamp. Shepton itself was never claimed as the birthplace, but in a custumal (a recital of the customs of the manor) dated 1575 I found the statement that Sir John Seymour had lived in the manor-house while he was Sheriff of Somerset in 1515-16. At that time his daughter Jane would have been some six years old and, with her brother Edward, the future duke of Somerset, may well have lived there with their father during his year of office.

As well as successes there were also disappointments. The delightful parish of Whitestaunton near Chard probably has as long a history of continuous occupation as almost any rural parish in the county. The remains of a Roman villa were discovered close to St Agnes's holy well, the parish church and the charming medieval manor-house. Sadly I arrived at Whitestaunton just a little too late. I was told that ten years earlier the Chard solicitors who had acted for the Elton family, former lords of the manor, had decided that their attic, in which their redundant records were stored, was a fire trap. The result was a bonfire which successfully wiped out much of the village's heritage.

There are so many memories of those days. I remember discovering with delight that in 1851 one third of the total population of Dowlish Wake, near Ilminster, then standing at 322, were surnamed Perry. The limited range of surnames at Merriott, near Crewkerne, in the early 17th century led certain individuals of the same names to adopt nicknames to differentiate between them: delightful names such as curlhead, noghead and boneback. Merriott, with a long history of market-gardening, also supplied in 1375 the earliest record of the English word 'nursery' for a garden.

The work of the *Victoria History of Somerset* proceeds. The fifth volume, covering the area to the west of the Quantocks was published in 1985; the sixth, by Dr Dunning and my successor, Mary Siraut, is to be devoted to the east of the Quantocks, including Bridgwater. It is eagerly awaited.

[97]

23
MONKSILVER AND MONKSILVER

EVERY now and then the past has a habit of obtruding on the present, particularly if one is an archivist. In August 1986 we bought a house. Not particularly out of the ordinary as houses go, but nice and, because it had to accommodate two libraries, large. It stood, indeed stands, on the north-east side of Taunton towards the far end of an unadopted cul-de-sac which in wet weather bears a strong resemblance to a swamp: namely Kilkenny Avenue. The numbering of the houses in this road has an idiosyncrasy which is all its own and reflects the order in which the buildings were put up. We are no.2 of a terrace of four known as Kilkenny Villas.

When an archivist buys an older house, natural curiosity inevitably leads him to find out about its past: who built it and what kind of people have made their respective homes beneath its roof. I was intrigued by the fact that our deeds showed that we were not allowed to 'erect or permit the erection of any Roman Catholick Church or any Roman Catholick institution' on any part of the premises; a condition which was the dreamchild of Jane Joanna Reeves, who sold the land for building in 1868. The buyer was property developer and auctioneer, Edwin Wotton, and the first of the four houses was completed in March 1870, ours being offered for letting on 7 October 1871. Wotton and his County Investment Company acted as landlords until they sold out to Robert Bruford in 1878.

The earliest individual I could trace who actually lived in the house was a Surveyor of Taxes, George Wright (1874-75), followed at intervals by the widow of a Collector for the Inland Revenue, Sarah Cornwall (1879-81), and the retired Taunton Divisional Engineer of the Great Western Railway, Thomas Hammett, who took up residence in 1881 and died in the house on 25 February 1904, aged 76. Among later occupiers was a former proprietor of hotels at Highbridge, Burnham and Yeovil, Charles Thomas Pitcher, who also passed away at Kilkenny in 1937, and Taunton's Prospective Parliamentary Labour Candidate, Sandra Horne (1975-77).

'Monksilver', Kilkenny Villas, Taunton: the joint home of Hilary, Robin, Catherine, Alexander and Tess (an extremely young Field Spaniel), not forgetting the Abbey National Building Society.

What really intrigued me, however, was that our house was the only one of the four to bear a name – Monksilver – the name also of a delightful village on the eastern flank of the Brendon Hills. Prolonged poring over rate books and directories eventually narrowed down the date of the house's christening to its purchase in 1945 by three spinster sisters, Clara, Mabel and Annie Poole. They ran a cafe and ironmongery in Station Road, Taunton, and one by one they died at the house: the last of them, Annie, as recently as 1970. Their obituaries in the local press indicated that all three had been born in Taunton and so I was no nearer to solving the origin of the house's name.

Further research identified the ladies' father as James Poole, a builder who had come to Taunton around 1880 and for many years ran a business in St Andrew's Road. I traced his burial in 1938, aged 75, in the registers of St Andrew's Church and, using that date, located his obituary in the *Somerset County Gazette.* This chronicled his career and added the key information that he had been born at – Monksilver !

As I often say when retelling this story, perhaps I should have left it there: but I didn't. I got out the Monksilver parish registers and easily located James's baptism on 20 April 1861. He was the youngest child of seven produced by George and Anne Poole. The father was described initially as a labourer, although later he was termed either as butcher or tailor. I noted that the eldest of George's offspring was named Matilda, baptised in 1842 and then, almost incidentally, I spotted that in 1865 she had an illegitimate child baptised named Arthur Harry, although no indication of the father's identity was given in the register. Little Arthur Harry was followed by little Clara, after whom one of my spinster sisters at Kilkenny Villas was probably named. And then Matilda really seems to have got the bit between her teeth, because she accumulated a further seven illegitimate children. These were all given rather more exotic names: Marmion, Mejiah, Maida, Minnie Marwood, Milo Marwood, Montague and Marwood.

I could not resist looking through the 1881 Census returns for Monksilver and, using these, I tracked down Matilda Poole living with her large brood at a house called Burfords. At this point I made a fascinating discovery. Matilda was described as the housekeeper and resident with her, recorded as head of the household and father of all Matilda's children was Mr Marwood Notley. Notley is a name to conjure with in the Monksilver area. The pub in the village has been called the Notley Arms since it changed its name from the Half Moon in the 1860s. The Notleys were lords of Monksilver manor and owned and occupied the nearby Tudor mansion called Combe Sydenham, former home of Sir Francis Drake's second wife and now open to the public.

Marwood had succeeded to the family estates on the death of his older brother, James Thomas Benedictus Notley, in 1851. The family pedigree in *Burke's Landed Gentry* indicates that Marwood never married and, when he died in 1903, his heirs were the children that he had produced by Matilda Poole. Papers in a solicitors' deposit at the Somerset Record Office showed that a number of the Poole children duly trotted off to change their surname by deeds poll to Notley and thus gained instant respectability. Of these, Montague and Marwood were

The Notley Arms, Monksilver, an excellent Somerset house for both food and liquid refreshment. It occurs as the Ram Inn by 1675, had become the Half Moon by 1785 and gained its present name c.1865. The Notley family had bought the neighbouring estate of Combe Sydenham in 1796 and four years later purchased the manor of Monksilver from the canons of Windsor. Their descendants hold the lordship of Monksilver to this day.

the principal beneficiaries and Combe Sydenham House was apparently only sold off after Marwood died in 1957.

The three spinster sisters who had moved into our house at Kilkenny Villas in 1945 were thus first cousins of the Pooles who had most fortuitously become Notleys. It at last become clear that they had chosen Monksilver as the name for our home not only because it had been their father's birthplace, but because it recalled for them what could arguably be hailed as the Pooles' finest hour.

There was a delightful postscript to this particular investigation. Recently there arrived at the Somerset Record Office a young South African gentleman who was trying to trace details of his great-grandfather. This ancestor, he told me, had eloped with a girl from Monksilver and married her on board the ship that carried them both out to South Africa. The name of his great-grandfather had been, he announced proudly, Milo Marwood Poole ! The story had come full circle.

24

LITTLE JACK HORNER

Pᴉᴄᴋ up almost any general book on Somerset and its history and you will find the claim that the original Little Jack Horner of nursery-rhyme fame was John Horner of Mells, who by underhand means obtained the deeds to Mells manor after the Dissolution of Glastonbury Abbey in 1539. It seems almost a shame to write *finis* to yet another delightful Somerset story, but the evidence does not bear out this colourful tale.

The character of Jack Horner is first found in an early 14th century ballad verse contained in a medieval manuscript in Cambridge University Library called 'the Tale of the Basyn'. This recounts how a priest was discovered with his lady friend by means of Jack Horner's miraculous bason. From this was derived the story of 'Jak and his Stepdame' and, by 1520, 'The Fryer and the Boy'. Henry Carey in his *Namby Pamby Ballads* of c.1720 wrote:

> Now he sings of Jacky Horner,
>   Sitting in the Chimney corner,
> Eating of a Christmas Pie,
>   Putting in his Thumb, Oh fie,
> Putting in, Oh fie ! his Thumb,
>   Pulling out, Oh Strange ! a Plum.

Jack next turns up in a chap book, first issued in 1764 and bearing the verbose title *The pleasant History of Jack Horner, Containing the witty Pranks he play'd from his Youth to his riper years, Being pleasant for Winter Evenings.*

The verses in this chap book cover twenty pages and make no reference to Somerset whatsoever. On the contrary they begin:

> Jack Horner was a pretty lad,
>   Near London he did dwell;
> His father's heart he made full glad,
>   His mother lov'd him well

The ballad continues:

THE
HISTORY
OF
JACK HORNER.

Containing,

The Witty Pranks he play'd,

From his YOUTH to his RIPER Years,

Being pleaſant for Winter Evenings.

Chapbook title-page, c.1770.

When friends they did together meet,
 To pass away the time,
Why little Jack be sure would eat
 His Christmas pye in rhyme.

And said Jack Horner, in the corner
 Eats good Christmas pye:
And with his thumbs pulls out the plumbs
 And said Good boy am I.

In the fulness of time Jack goes out to service with a brave knight, plays a prank with his miraculous bason, slays a terrible giant and finally marries the knight's daughter.

The rhyme was probably first linked with Somerset in the 18th century. The Horners of Mells were the only prominent English family to bear that surname and a story clearly evolved to fit the verse. The tale occurs in its final form in the Rev F.W. Cleverdon's *History of Mells*, published in 1974. 'Thomas [sic John?] Horner, entrusted with the surrendered deeds of Glastonbury Abbey, on his way to London to deliver them to Cromwell, took for himself the deeds of Mells from the pie in which they were hidden. The plum was the Manor.'

The home of the Horners. Mells Manor House, 1885, probably built by John Selwood, abbot of Glastonbury 1456-92, but much added to in the 16th century. It was described as partly ruinous in 1794 but was restored by the Horners c.1900.

Mells manor, with many other estates, was acquired from the Crown in 1543 by Thomas (later Sir Thomas) Horner and his brother, John, not by illicitly pocketing title-deeds but by handing over the then phenomenal sum of £1,831 19s 11 ¼d. Sir Thomas Horner's will, proved in 1555, indicates that the property was bought by the two brothers with Sir Thomas's money and then leased to Sir Thomas by John Horner and his son Robert (who died in 1551). In the will the Mells estate was left to John's son, Sir John Horner, High Sheriff of Somerset in 1564 and 1573, who died in 1587.

Mells continued in the Horner family until Katharine Frances, daughter of a much later Sir John Horner, brought it to the family of her husband, Raymond Asquith, eldest son of the Prime Minister. Following Raymond Asquith's death on the Somme in 1916 it passed to his son Julian, 2nd Earl of Oxford and Asquith.

The story of Little Jack Horner is just that – a story.

25
SIMPLY RIPPING!

IN 1911 air-race fever swept across Britain. It was less than eight years since the Wright brothers had made the first powered flight and most of the population had yet to catch even a glimpse of the flimsy wire-and-wood flying machines. *The Daily Mail* put up the very considerable prize of £10,000 to be competed for over a triangular course, from Brooklands to Edinburgh then to Exeter and back to Brooklands. A vast crowd of 250,000 cheered the 20 competitors off on 22 July and, of these, three British aviators crashed even before the first short hop to Hendon was completed.

There was one Somerset entrant, Collyns Price Pizey, aged 27. He had been born at Clevedon and educated at Dawlish, King's College, Taunton, and at Salisbury. After employment with an engineering firm, he had developed an interest in flying, although he had taken his first lesson as recently as the previous January, going solo only three days later. He declared that his first impression of flight was that 'he wanted to blow his nose and couldn't'. Sadly Pizey went out in the early stages with a forced landing at Melton Mowbray.

Aviation was a dangerous occupation in those early days, although fortunately there were no fatalities in the Great Race itself. The course took its toll on the machines, however, and after Edinburgh the contenders were down to only four: two French and two English. Both Frenchmen were way out in front when they touched down at Filton aerodrome near Bristol on the evening of 25 July. The leader, Lt Jean Conneau, masquerading under his 'flying name' of Andre Beaumont, was greeted by an enormous crowd which mobbed his Bleriot monoplane, after which he was driven to the Clifton Downs Hotel: duly followed by his compatriot, Mons Vedrines.

The telephone wires from Bristol rapidly became red hot to ensure that the people of Somerset were ready to greet the valiant birdmen on the following morning. Indeed, many never went to bed at all. The Bristol take-off was delayed until 4.45 am because a low mist hung over the area. It was anticipated that the aircraft would follow the GWR line down to Exeter, and so it proved. The cliffs above Cheddar were crowded to see the Frenchmen pass. The people of Bridgwater gathered on the Mump near the docks, while as many as possible packed themselves onto the top of St Mary's tower. Others pedalled furiously on their bikes out to the Polden Hills or streamed out of town on foot to Wembdon Hill and Bath Road Bridge, where over 1,000 gathered. After a false alarm at 4 am, due to two high-flying birds, the aeroplanes were seen approaching over Woolavington. 'The noise of the engine could be distinctly heard and the propeller could be seen whizzing round ... The crowd went into quite an ecstasy of delight' and cheered as Vedrines passed above them.

At Taunton the crowds began to assemble on Stonegallows Hill from 3 am, the first car to arrive being driven by Mr Marshalsea of East Street. 'Several who had overslept themselves appeared without collars and in their slippers', while at 5.30 am Mr A.G. Palmer, Chief of the Taunton Fire Brigade, turned up to announce the exact time that the planes had left Bristol. The fliers appeared soon after, remaining in sight of the rapt onlookers for nearly five minutes. At Wellington most of the populace had headed up the Blackdowns to the Monument, leaving the less energetic to settle for the Church Fields. Similar crowds turned out across South Somerset as the aircraft sped back from Exeter, heading for the next control point on Salisbury Plain. All the engine drivers at Yeovil Junction 'tooted' their locomotive whistles as Vedrines flew over them, although it was Beaumont who made it back first to Brooklands to scoop the prize at an average speed of 45 mph.

There were still two English pilots in the race, although they were some way behind – in fact, a whole week behind ! The Press could only praise their 'dogged determination'. James Valentine had to fly very low over Bridgwater on 2 August because of fog and cloud, and on the return leg from Exeter he had to land near Bruton for two hours to get his bearings. He was to win a gold cup as the first British pilot to finish. His problems, however, were few compared with those of Samuel Cody, who brought up the rear a day later.

Cody, dubbed 'the erratic and tardy aviator', lost his way soon after taking off from Filton and found himself over Weston-super-Mare. After circling above Ellenborough Park, he dropped down in front of the Grand Atlantic Hotel. Narrowly missing the seafront wall, he landed his biplane on the beach, avoiding with difficulty a number of kites which were being flown, not to mention a multitude of deckchairs. He was then hurried onto the Pier where he addressed an attentive audience of some

Mr B.C. Hucks soars above Burnham sea-front in his Blackburn monoplane, 1911 (from a photograph).

5,000. His troubles were still not over for, on the return leg towards Salisbury, he mistook Bristol for Bath and landed at Hanham, unconvincingly blaming a faulty compass. Although he eventually completed the course, he was to die tragically only two years later in a flying accident at Farmborough.

This brief taste of aviation only left the people of Somerset wanting more. The services of a Blackburn pilot, Mr B.C. Hucks, were obtained for a 'Coronatia Fete' in Taunton's Vivary Park on 7 August. When it was found that he had insufficient room to take off, the beefiest of the spectators carried his 'Mercury' biplane bodily over hedges and across fields to the top of Cotlake Hill near Trull. His flying demonstration ended with a landing in Ash Meadows. Seeing that his plane was going to crash into some iron railings before he could stop it, the intrepid aviator leaped from his bucket seat and ran backwards in front of it, trying to halt the aircraft's progress. In these valiant efforts he was only partially successful and emergency repairs at Messrs Beach's Motor Works in St James Street proved necessary.

From Taunton Mr Hucks proceeded to Burnham where he made display flights from Pillsmouth Farm on 16 and 17 August, tossing out bundles of scrap paper in mid-air to enchant his public. Such was his popularity that the Highbridge Adult School Horticultural Show, held simultaneously, made an unexpected loss. Thence Hucks flew to Minehead where he took Charles Forrest's black terrier pup aloft as a passenger. On one of a number of flights there, he landed at Dunster in the middle of a polo match, from which Mr Geoffrey Luttrell bore him off in triumph to Dunster Castle for afternoon tea. Early in September

Hucks transferred to Weston-super-Mare whence he flew across the Bristol Channel, circled Cardiff and returned.

Hucks did not have it all his own way. Graham Gilmour appeared at the Yeovil Friendly Society Fete on 8 August. Gilmour was only one of three aviators expected on the following day at the Martock, Ash and Long Load Flower, Fruit, Vegetable and Honey Show – try getting that on a poster ! In the event only Gilmour turned up, one of the others, Mr Morison, having smashed his undercarriage at Maidenhead. Gilmour's aircraft was owned by the British and Colonial Aeroplane Co (later the Bristol Aeroplane Co), who charged their Martock devotees the considerable sum of £111 for his appearance. The show still managed to clear a substantial profit. Gilmour subsequently based his machine at Bower Hinton Farm, Martock, in a field that is still called Aerodrome, although only six month's later he was another early aviator to be killed, when the wing of his aeroplane collapsed.

The Gilmour machine had one advantage over Hucks's plane in that it could carry human passengers, albeit one by one. On the day of the show a series of shuttle flights between Martock and Stoke-sub-Hamdon started, the first intrepid volunteer being Dr Ingle of Somerton. Other brave souls from Langport, Yeovil, Bridgwater and Martock itself followed, heartened by the safe return of the good doctor. Only one lady was among those who ventured that day on Somerset's first short-lived passenger air service: an American visitor, Miss McLaughlin. On her descent to terra firma she announced with glee that it had been 'simply ripping !' Her remark succinctly summed up Somerset's joyous reaction to the dawn of air travel.

Graham Gilmour in his Bristol Boxkite: the first commercially-produced aircraft in England.

26

THE SEA-FARING BIGAMIST

PEOPLE who look into their ancestry do not always find the forebears that they expect. Stories handed down from generation to generation are liable to become exaggerated, particularly when, as in this instance, the descendants grew up on the other side of the world.

In 1973 an enquiry arrived in Somerset from Queensland in Australia from the granddaughter of William Field Barnard, born at Somerton in 1842. According to the lady, Barnard was son of Capt. Charles Matthew Barnard, RN, by his wife, Betsy Field. There was a tradition in the family of a coat of arms of a demi-bear rampant with the motto 'Fer et Perfer' – 'bear and forebear': both clearly intended to be a rather tortuous pun on the name Barnard. Initial searches revealed the crest of a demi-bear and the motto as stated as having been borne by Fulke Lancelot Wade Barnard of Portishead in Somerset, although no evidence was found of Captain Charles Matthews Barnard at Somerton.

A second letter from the same correspondent landed on my desk nine years later. Further research had traced the birth at Somerton on 13 December 1841 of William Field, illegitimate son of Betsy Barnard. Even more telling was the marriage there, a year before on 1 December 1840 of Charles Butt, gent., bachelor, and Betsy Barnard, spinster, daughter of William Barnard, gent. More telling because in the margin was added 'Charles Butt was subsequently convicted of bigamy at the Somerset Quarter Sessions'.

The case was tried at Quarter Sessions in January 1842, evidence having been taken from witnesses the previous October. Charles Butt was described as aged 29, 'a young man of somewhat gentlemanly dress and appearance with good features'. He was certainly not a Captain in the Royal Navy but a master mariner from Southampton, although born on the Isle of Wight. Testimony indicated that he had been married in 1834 at St George in the East, Middlesex, to Mary Field, niece of Thomas Flint Field of Hutton, Essex, esq. By her Butt had two daughters, only one of which, Ellen, survived. He evidently deserted his wife Mary in Jersey, and turned up at Somerton in May 1840.

St Michael's Church, Somerton, where Charles Butt illegally plighted his troth.

In Somerset he passed himself off as a naval Captain with an estate worth £300 a year, £1,000 worth of timber, a mansion and farmhouse and shares in ships. In no time at all his grey eyes and fresh complexion had won over old Mrs Keturah Barnard, followed quickly by her 26-year-old daughter, Betsy, and, in seven months, by matrimony. Unfortunately for Betsy, by the time Charles's guilty secret leaked out, she was already pregnant.

Witnesses to both marriages were shipped in to Taunton Castle to testify at Charles Butt's trial, although Charles's sister, Jane Gillespie, absconded from the George Inn at Bridgwater after her arrival from London. Among those called was Betsy's mother, 'a venerable old lady in a state of great apparent distress', who plaintively stated that her daughter 'was confined not long since, and she and the child are so ill that we have little hope of saving either of them'. Charles was duly convicted of bigamy and sentenced to 18 months hard labour. The local newspaper commented that he was already 'undergoing his expiatory daily performance on the tread mill' at Wilton Gaol in Taunton.

The Barnards succeeded in marrying off Betsy to local farmer, Michael Dawe of East Chinnock, in 1846, with whom she began to raise a new family. Little William Field Barnard lived with them for a while, but his presence evidently constituted a perpetual embarrassment and he was eventually packed off to Australia. There he managed to start life afresh and spread the name of Barnard even further.

There are two rather intriguing footnotes to this story. We have already met Thomas Flint Field, uncle of Charles Butt's first wife, Mary. Thomas's son, William Ventris Field, became a successful barrister, Justice of the Queen's Bench, Privy Councillor and, in 1890, was created Baron Field of Bakeham. He died in 1907 aged 93, worth over £85,000: first cousin by marriage to a conman, common sailor and bigamist.

The second footnote appeared in the *Taunton Courier* for 16 August 1843. It read 'Charles Butt, calling himself Captain Butt, a few weeks ago completed his term of 18 months hard labour in Wilton Gaol. This heartless fellow, on leaving his prison, took up his abode at a public house in this town [Taunton] and last week went off with the landlord's wife, the latter having taken with her upwards of £40'. By way of explanation, the paper added that 'the personal appearance of the villain was rather pleasing'.

Somerset never heard of him again.

27

THE MISTLETOE BOUGH

THE small village of Bawdrip, a little over three miles north-east of Bridgwater, cherishes a tragic story of a young bride who died on her wedding day: a bride immortalised by a Victorian parlour song.

According to the words of T.H. Bayly, set to music by Sir H.R. Bishop –

> The mistletoe hung in the castle hall,
> 　The holly branch shone on the old oak wall
> And the baron's retainers were blithe and gay,
> 　And keeping their Christmas holiday.
> The Baron beheld with a father's pride
> 　His beautiful child, young Lovell's bride,
> The star of the goodly company
>
> I'm weary of dancing now, she cried,
> 　Here tarry a moment, I'll hide, I'll hide,
> And Lovell be sure thou'rt the first to trace
> 　The clue to my secret hiding place.
>
> Away she ran and her friends began
> 　Each tower to search and each nook to scan,
> And young Lovell cried, Oh where dost thou hide ?
> 　I'm lonesome without thee, my own dear bride.
>
> They sought her that night, and they sought her next day,
> 　They sought her in vain while a week passed away;
> In the highest, the lowest, the loneliest spot,
> 　Young Lovell sought wildly, but found her not.
> And years flew by, and their grief at last
> 　Was told as a sorrowful tale long past ...
>
> At length an oak chest that had long lain hid
> 　Was found in the castle; they raised the lid,
> And a skeleton form lay mouldering there
> 　In the bridal wreath of that lady fair ...

Oh, sad was her fate, in sportive jest
She hid from her lord in the old oak chest.
It closed with a spring and her bridal bloom
Lay withering there in a living tomb.

Arthur Mee's *Somerset* (1940) records that the bride of the Mistletoe Bough was Eleanor Lovell, daughter of the rector of Bawdrip. She crept into a chest to hide on her wedding day and found herself a prisoner. There 'the bride lay while all around the search went on, and no one heard her cries. The tragedy was complete, and not for years, when the old chest was opened by another generation, was the missing bride discovered.'

The story is an old one and appeared as the tale of Ginevra, a bride who died under exactly the same circumstances in Samuel Rogers's poem, *Italy* (1822-28). Rogers noted 'The story is, I believe, founded on fact; though the time and place are uncertain. Many old houses lay claim to it.'

The events were linked with Bawdrip because of the name Lovell and a tombstone in the chancel behind the altar. Of course, in the song Lovell was the name of the bridegroom not the bride. The tombstone commemorates the Rev Edward Lovell, his wife Eleanor, both from Batcombe, and their two daughters, Mary and Eleanor. The father was rector of Bawdrip for 14 years but his wife and elder daughter died before him. The latin inscription records that 'Eleanor, the daughter, heiress of the family honour and estates, died June 14th 1681. Her sorrowing husband mourned her, taken away by a sudden and untimely fate soon after the marriage celebrations' and her husband erected the monument.

One problem is that the Bawdrip parish registers do not survive from as far back as 1681. It proved possible, however, to trace the marriage licence for the wedding of Eleanor Roberts of Bawdrip, widow, and the Rev Thomas Holt, rector of Bawdrip, issued on 18 April 1681, a full two months before the date of Eleanor's death. As marriages were almost invariably solemnized within a few days of the granting of the licence, Eleanor's death on her wedding day seems highly unlikely. Her first husband was the Rev Thomas Roberts, Holt's predecessor as rector of Bawdrip, who had died in, or shortly before, February 1681. Eleanor thus appears to have remarried with almost unseemly haste, only months after the death of her first husband.

The facts, therefore, do not coincide with those of the song in any

St Michel's Church, Bawdrip, housing the controversial Lovell memorial.

respect. Eleanor did not marry a Lovell, nor live in a castle. She was not a young bride but a widow and she probably died not on her wedding day but weeks after her second marriage.

Intriguingly the true story plays its part in revealing an extremely elaborate hoax. In 1974 there appeared from the pen of one Edward Ryall a 200-page book entitled *Second Time Round*, which purported to be the autobiographical reminiscences of the 17th century John Fletcher of Westonzoyland – Ryall claiming to be Fletcher's reincarnation.

Ryall, as Fletcher, narrated that in 1679 Eleanor Lovell began 'walking out' with Mark Fowler, a farmer's son from Chedzoy, and that they were married on 14 June 1681. The disappearance of the bride on her wedding day is then recounted, as in the song. As we have seen, Eleanor was still married to the Rev Thomas Roberts in 1679 and she married, in 1681, not Mark Fowler but the Rev Thomas Holt. There are several other historical innaccuracies in Ryall's work which establish it as a work of clever fiction rather than inspired fact.

We will probably never know the truth about Eleanor's sudden and untimely death: a fatal fall, a tragic childbirth or a sudden illness. We can, however, be fairly sure that she did not breathe her last in a locked chest.

28

THE MILLER'S TALE

IN an age when divorce was possible only by Act of Parliament at considerable expense, and thus reserved for the wealthy, the poor evolved a safety valve for unhappy marriages: the wife sale. In their innocence they believed such a transaction had the force of law and during the 18th and early 19th centuries practised it widely. Such a bargain featured in Thomas Hardy's novel, *The Mayor of Casterbridge*, and similar sales formed the subject of a recent book.

While working on the papers of the Trollope-Bellew family of Crowcombe, held at the Somerset Record Office, I came across a paper which actually documented such a sale.

MEMORANDUM

I, John Bodger, this eighth day of November 1761 have and do and for divers good causes and lawful reasons moving me thereunto let and set and entirely sell all my right and property in Betty Bolt otherwise Betty Bodger, my lawful wife, as it appears by the register of the parish church of Taunton St. James in the County of Somerset, unto James Bacon of the parish of Stogursey, fisherman, to have and to hold as his lawful wife for evermore. And I, the said John Bodger, do promise and assure the said James Bacon that, on the penalty or forfeiture of £10 of good and lawful money of Great Britain, I will never claim or make any demand or demands on the said Betty Bolt or her new husband the aforesaid James Bacon.

In witness whereof we have hereunto set our hands and seals the day and year above written

John Bodger X his mark
James Bacon X his mark
Betty Bolt X her mark

It was a comparatively straightforward exercise to confirm that John Bodger and Betty Bolt had indeed been married at Taunton St James in

1746, 15 years before, and that James Bacon's first wife, Jane, had died in 1759. Then came the real surprise, for James Bacon and Betty Bodger were married at Stogursey two years after the 'sale', in 1763. The church had sanctioned this rural divorce. And little Betty came along in 1764!

The choicest example of a Somerset wife sale, however, was the one which I managed to reconstruct from parish poor-law records. Coincidentally it happened quite close to the area of Betty Bolt's goings-on. William Bacon, a farm labourer and no relation to the above James, was born at Sampford Arundel in 1725. When he was 15 he hired himself to John Tonkins of St Decuman's for 50s. (£2.50) a year and in 1748 he got Mary Gadd of Stogumber pregnant. The Stogumber overseers of the poor, having evidently failed to persuade Bacon to marry Mary while sober, managed to get him drunk and carried him to Stogumber church, 'very high in liquor', for the ceremony. Bacon subsequently took to his heels and fled, probably never seeing his own little Betty Bacon who was christened three months after the wedding.

Bacon's wife, Mary, alone with a young child, eventually moved in with labourer Robert Jones and, from 1757 had a further ten children by him, all illegitimate. Meanwhile William Bacon had crossed the Quantocks and found work in Bridgwater. Fortune took him to nearby Durleigh and then, in 1780, over 30 years after his enforced marriage, he

Stogumber village, where in December 1784 William Bacon sold his wife and four children to Robert Jones for five shillings.

[TO WIT.] } To the churchwardens and overseers of the poor of the parish - of *Stogumber* ——— in the said *County* — and to the churchwardens and overseers of the poor of the parish —— of *Spaxton* — — — — ——— in the said *County* — and to each and every of them.

UPON the complaint of the churchwardens and overseers of the poor of the parish ——— of *Stogumber* ——— aforesaid in the said *County* - of *Somerset* ——— unto us whose names are hereunto set and seals affixed, being two of his majesty's justices of the peace in and for the said *county* ——— of *Somerset* ——— and one of us of the quorum, that *William Bacon Mary his Wife Mary their Daughter aged 20 years Robert their Son aged 17 years Jane their Daughter aged 13 years & Samuel their Son aged 9 years* —— have come to inhabit in the said *parish* —— of *Stogumber* ——— not having gained a legal settlement there, nor produced any certificate owning *them or any of them* ——— to be settled elsewhere, and that the said *William Bacon Mary his Wife Mary Robert Jane & Samuel their Children are* —— likely to be chargeable to the said *parish* —— of *Stogumber* ——— ; We the said justices upon due proof made thereof, as well upon examination of the said *William Bacon* —— ——— upon oath, as otherwise, and likewise upon due consideration had of the premisses, do adjudge the same to be true; and we do likewise adjudge, that the lawful settlement of *them* the said *William Bacon Mary his Wife Mary Robert Jane & Samuel their Children* ——— is in the said *parish* - of *Spaxton* — — — — in the said *County* of *Somerset* — — We do therefore require you the said churchwardens and overseers of the poor of the said *parish* - of *Stogumber* ——— or some, or one of you, to convey the said *William Bacon Mary his Wife Mary Robert Jane & Samuel their Children* — — — from and out of your said *parish* of *Stogumber* ——— to the said *parish* - of *Spaxton* - — — — ——— and *them* — to deliver to the churchwardens and overseers of the poor there, or to some, or one of them, together with this our order, or a true copy thereof; And we also hereby require you the said churchwardens and overseers of the poor of the said *parish* of *Spaxton* —— ——— to receive and provide for *them* as ——— inhabitants of your *parish*. —— Given under our hands and seals the *Twentieth* day *of December* in the year of our Lord one thousand seven hundred and *Eighty four*

Settlement removal order for William Bacon, his wife and four children from Stogumber to Spaxton, 1784.

rented a set of mills at Spaxton from Richard Kidner for eight years at 16gns. (£16.80) a year. This act obtained for him a new settlement and meant that if the Stogumber overseers found him they could remove Mary, still his lawful wife, and her children, nominally Bacon's as her husband, to Spaxton where they would become a charge on that parish's poor rates.

William had not been any more celibate than Mary. By his new girlfriend, Elizabeth, he had at least three children baptised at Durleigh as legitimate. Word of Bacon's rise in the world almost inevitably reached the Stogumber parish officers. By this time one of Mary's daughters was about to produce her own illegitimate child, who would take the place of her birth as her settlement and thus become a permanent charge on Stogumber parish. The overseers therefore prepared to remove Mary and four of her younger children to Spaxton.

William Bacon was clearly horrified at this turn of events and arranged to meet Robert Jones at Stogumber where in 1784, five days before Christmas, he solemnly sold his wife and four children to Jones for 5s.(£0.25) and then went home to his Spaxton mill.

The authorities were determined not to have their plans foiled in this manner and knew that they had to work fast before the illegitimate grandchild was born. They hauled William before the Justices and on 11 January 1785 obtained a removal order for the husband, wife Mary, and her children: Mary (20), then 'big with child', Robert (17), Jane (13) and Samuel (9). That they finally succeeded is shown by the christening at Spaxton in March 1785 of Robert, base born son of Mary Bacon *alias* Jones. The saga clearly continued, for in 1798 a bastardy order was imposed at Spaxton on Robert Jones otherwise Bacon for the maintenance of a female bastard born on the body of Jane Bartram. His indiscretion was to cost Robert £1 down and a further 1s. (£0.05) a week.

The Somerset magistrates had shown that might was right and that they were not to be trifled with.

29
STONE GALLOWS

THE traveller heading west from Taunton towards Wellington and Exeter along the A 38 passes through a hamlet called Stone Gallows and past a restaurant of the same name. Towards the top of the hill the main road sweeps to the left, but before the present century it continued along what is now only a narrow lane leading to the village of Rumwell. On a triangle of waste ground, at a T-junction near the brow of the hill, once stood the gallows which gave its hated name to that area.

The name of the gallows was apparently derived from a great boulder which in turn christened the nearby Stone Green; not because the gibbet was made of stone, as suggested by the nearby innsign. The site was chosen because the gallows were regarded as unclean and the spot lay on a 'no-man's-land' at the junction of three parishes: Bishops Hull, Trull and Wilton.

The bishops of Winchester, lords of Taunton Deane manor by the 10th century, claimed the right to raise their own gallows as early as 1275, and their records mention several executions during the medieval period. These hangings very probably occurred at Stone Gallows but the earliest specific reference is found in a petition of 1615 which states that the gallows were certainly in use by about 1575 and that the parishes of Bishops Hull and Trull had been jointly responsible 'tyme out of mynde ... for the mendinge and new makinge of forches [an old word for gallows] standinge at Stone in the tithinge of Rumwell when and as often as neade did require'. A dispute had arisen as to the relative liabilities of the two parishes and Trull had refused to contribute. One witness claimed that Bishops Hull men had usually gone into Trull parish and demanded a tree with which to build the gallows, while another asserted that two trees had been felled at Bishops Hull in recent years for the same purpose.

The earliest account of an execution which referred to Stone Gallows was that of three men and a woman who had murdered the curate of Old Cleeve as he travelled along the highway. This ruthless quartet,

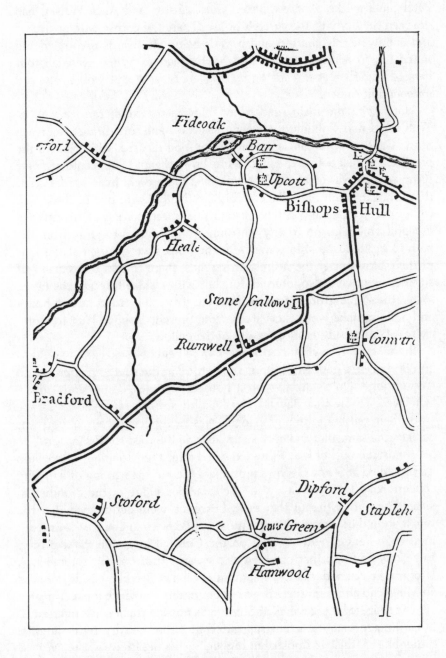

Location of Stone Gallows, near Bishops Hull village, from a map of 1791.

Peter Smethwicke, Andrew Baker, Cyril Austen and Alice Walker, had dragged the body to the curate's house. There the corpse was 'quartered and imboweld, his quarters and bowels being afterwards perboyled and salted up, in a most strange and fearful manner'. They were all four hanged together at 11 am on 24 July 1624 and 'dyed obstinate and unrepenting sinners'.

Until 1752 the main road from Taunton to Exeter ran by way of Trull Road and Galmington, over the little Ramshorn Bridge, to reach Stone Gallows by an ancient route, now long disused, which joined the present A38 just before the gibbet site. From the mid 18th century a new turnpike road was created which followed the present main road, except that it ran through the village of Bishops Hull. Along one of these two routes every criminal was taken by horse and cart, sitting on his coffin; a dreadful object lesson to any who might be tempted to stray from the path of righteousness. In some cases the bodies were buried at the foot of the gallows or at the nearest crossroads, there to join the remains of suicides who were also interred thus but with a stake through the heart. When the Wellington New Road was constructed in 1838 human bones and a stout stake were excavated at the present Bishops Hull to Comeytrowe crossroads, east of the site of the gallows.

In the early 18th century prisoners were held until execution at Taunton Bridewell, a gaol which until 1754 stood at the southern approach to Tone Bridge. On 23 April 1709 it housed two men, Trood and Tidball, who were to die that day at Stone Gallows. Both managed to escape from their cell but, although Tidball was never seen again, Trood was retaken the same day and duly swung beside the road to Wellington.

A mistaken belief that those executed after the Monmouth Rebellion of 1685 died at Stone Gallows presumably led to the naming of a nearby modern road Jeffreys Way, after the infamous judge of the Bloody Assizes. The authorities of that time, however, were determined that the rebels should be executed in the most public place in Taunton. Nineteen men were hanged without trial on the Cornhill (now the Parade) on 9 July 1685 and a further nineteen at the same spot on 19 September. A later source claimed that those sentenced died at Pen Elm beside the road to Minehead although there is no contemporary evidence for such a site.

The shape of the gallows at Stone was not the traditional inverted 'L' but a long horizontal beam supported at either end by two uprights: rather like football goalposts but higher. Such a design was necessary for multiple executions, as on 2 April 1718 when Isaac Robbins, Richard

Bartlet, John Chilcot and John Cooksey were hoisted aloft together. Single victims were more usual, however, as when Nathaniel Withyman of Ashill was convicted of murdering his employer, Farmer Trott, in a quarrel over Withyman's sweetheart. He was drawn from the town bound to a sledge and hanged on 21 April 1738.

At the Taunton Assizes of 1741 nine men received sentence of death but one of these was helped by his wife to take poison 'in order, as he foolishly said, that the court should not have their ends of him'. One other, who had murdered a glover, 'wishing when he was taken up that if he was guilty his legs might rot off, met with such a judgement, for his legs actually rotted off at the small [of his back], and he was carried in a chair to receive his sentence. He is to be hang'd in chains.' The punishment of hanging in chains was reserved for the worst crimes, when a lasting object lesson had to be given to the people. While the criminal was awaiting execution he was measured by a blacksmith who then forged a cage-like framework from narrow bands of iron. This fitted closely round the head, body and sometimes limbs of the felon's corpse, and was then suspended from the gibbet at the execution site for months or even years, supporting the body even after it had decomposed.

In 1758 the victims were two soldiers who had murdered a woman in Bath while trying to escape from the bridewell there, and who were brought all the way to Taunton Assizes before paying the ultimate penalty on 4 April. Another Bath man, Richard Gulliver, was condemned for the murder of his wife, 'behaved penitent and confessed the fact', and was hanged on 1 April 1769.

As the century wore on, the last remains of those executed were often put to a practical use and delivered to local surgeons for dissection. The knowledge that their punishment was to extend beyond the grave must have given an added dimension of horror to Nehemiah Webber and Stephen Scadding, as they stood at Stone Gallows with the halters about their necks on 26 April 1770, following the murder of a gentleman's servant near Taunton. At least one highwayman is known to have choked his life away on Stone Gallows: William Lattmore on 17 April 1783, followed by a 34-year-old horse thief, John Lewis, on 10 April 1788. While Lewis was confessing his crime in the execution cart a young charcoal burner, John Walford, stole a knife below the gallows. A year later it became a murder weapon when Walford slew his young wife.

Occasionally criminals were executed near the scene of their crime, although even then tradition demanded that the hanging be on common or waste ground. On the same day that Lewis was suspended at Stone Gallows, Samuel Yandall was hanged at Dodhill Green beside the road from Taunton to Kingston St Mary for the burglary of nearby Pyrland Hall.

Although so many crimes then carried the death penalty, many of those tried at the Assize Hall in Taunton Castle and found guilty of lesser felonies than murder were often reprieved. For murder itself there was no reprieve. On 1 April 1792 Job Bowden from Mark, aged 32, ended his days at Stone Gallows for the murder of his mother Elizabeth in a drunken fit, although he 'denied the fact to the last moment'. A year later on 3 April 1793 Joan Tottle, a 29-year-old spinster, was hanged for murdering her illegitimate child at West Monkton. As the local paper commented, 'she seemed but little concerned at her approaching dissolution, but at the place of execution she appeared penitent, acknowledged her guilt, and hoped all young women will take warning by her shameful and untimely end'. A wife murderer followed on 31 March 1794: Thomas Withys, aged only 24, who had drowned his spouse Mary in a pond at Pilton, and freely admitted the deed. In 1798 two men died as the result of a squabble over three and a half guineas (£3.67½). John Isaacs, aged 38 and born at White Lackington, murdered the Bath bailiff who was taking his goods for unpaid rent. At Stone Gallows on 2 April 1798 'he acknowledged the justness of his untimely end, but seemed little affected at his awful situation even to the last'.

There was one particular hanging-day, however, which became part of the folklore of Somerset; a day when no fewer than nine men were hanged together. Years afterwards John Masey, a Bishops Hull builder,

> Wednesday last was executed at Stone gallows, near Taunton, John Isaacs, a resident for these last fourteen years at Bath, for the wilful murder of John Wilmot, a bailiff; that was taking a distress of three guineas and half for rent. He acknowledged the justness of his untimely end, but seemed little affected at his awful situation even to the last; aged 37.

Account of the execution of John Isaacs in 1798.

Wednesday nine prisoners were executed at Stone Gallows, near Taunton, pursuant to their sentences, viz. Samuel Tout, otherwise Greenslade, aged about 35, and Robert Westcott, aged about 30 both labourers, for entering the dwelling-house of Richard Griffey, a baker, of Old Cleve, and causing thirty loaves of bread to be disposed of at 10d. each. Both admitted they had the loaves, but Tout denied to the last ever having the pickaxe in his hand with which the baker's door was forced open, as was sworn on the trial, and there is reason to believe it was another person, who has absconded. The other sufferers were George Tout, William Warry, and Edward Jeffery, for sheep-stealing; Robert Dee, alias Williams, alias Brown, for stealing a box of lace; Robert Wygood, for stealing a canvas bag containing about 30l.! Michael Day, for stealing a cart-mare; and Peter Kingdon, for stealing two heifers and a steer. They all behaved very penitently. It being apprehended that some riotous proceedings might take place, parties of horse and foot soldiers attended the execution, and not the least disturbance happened.

Newspaper description of the day on which nine men were hanged together at Stone Gallows in 1801.

and George Dudderidge of Allerford recalled how on 15 April 1801 the 'nine poor fellows' were driven from prison to Bishops Hull, sitting on their coffins and guarded by mounted dragoons. 'The nine ropes for hanging were suspended from an erected gallows; as the ropes were placed around the necks of the men the cart was drawn away from under them, and they were left suspended'. It is often stated that all nine were convicted for stealing bread, but in fact only two of the sufferers were linked with the bread riots of that year.

The names and offences of the nine criminals were as follows: Edward Jeffery, aged 49 from Chardstock, for sheepstealing; William Warry, also aged 49 from Chardstock, for the same crime; Robert Weygood, aged 26 from Milverton, for burgling the house of Mr G. Hancock and stealing a canvas bag containing £30; George Tout *alias* Greenslade, aged 27 from Upton, for stealing wheat; William Tout, aged 26 from Wiveliscombe,

33 William Warry born at ~~Milverton~~ Chardstock in this County was Executed at Stone Gallows near Taunton April 15th 1801 Aged 49 for Sheep Stealing. Acknowledg'd his guilt

37 Robt Weygood born at Milverton in this County was Executed at Stone Gallows near Taunton April 15th 1801 (for Burglary in the House of G. Hancock) Aged 36.
Confess'd himself guilty of the Crime

40 George Tout alias Greenslade born at Upton in this County was Executed at Stone Gallows April 15th 1801 Aged 27 for Stealing Wheat. Confess'd his guilt

41 William Tout born at Wivelscombe in this County was Executed at Stone Gallows April 15 1801 Aged 26 for Rioting and forcibly taking bread out of a Bakers Shop.
Deny'd the Crime for which he suffer'd

42 John Westcote born at Williton in this County was Executed at Stone Gallows April 15th 1801 Aged 23 for Rioting as above
Deny'd the Crime, alledging that he pray'd for the riot

43 Robert Deo alias Williams alias Brown born on the Sea of German Parents, was Executed at Stone Gallows April 15th 1801 Aged 24 for Burglary. Acknowledg'd his guilt

The gaol chaplain notes executions at Stone Gallows in 1801.

and John Westcote, aged 23 from Withycombe, for rioting, breaking open Richard Griffey's bakery at Old Cleeve, and forcing Mrs Griffey to sell them 30 loaves at the reduced price of 10d each (about 4p) instead of 1s 6d (7½p); Robert Deo *alias* Williams *alias* Brown, aged 24, born at sea of German parents, for burglary and stealing a box of lace; Peter Kingdon, aged 22 from Withycombe, for stealing two heifers and a steer; Michael Day, aged 46 from Holton, for stealing a cart mare. All confessed their guilt with the exception of William Tout, who claimed to the last that he paid for the bread. In August 1829 one of the nine horses that drew the nine men to their sad end was still proudly exhibited at Pool Farm, south of Taunton, at the considerable age of 33.

Only very seldom are details given of the scene at the execution. In the late 18th and early 19th centuries there was no gaol chaplain at Taunton and from 1789 all executions at Stone Gallows were attended by the 'ordinary' or chaplain from Ilchester gaol, the Rev Thomas Gwynne Rees. His notebook survives, listing all the hangings at which he officiated and including the texts of his exhortations to the condemned. It contains the following cautionary verse he penned in 1803.

> *'He that once sins, like him that slides on ice,*
> *Glides swiftly down the slipp'ry paths of vice,*
> *He sees the danger which he ought to shun,*
> *But presses on though sure to be undone.'*

It was not until the mid 19th century that one hangman served most of England: men such as William Calcraft and William Marwood. Earlier each Assize town seems to have had its own. At Ilchester successive members of the Mitchell family of Long Load 'turned off' those condemned. At Taunton a single family supplied the town with hangmen for at least four generations, as described by a visitor in 1804.

'Here is a poor devil named Joshua Otway, great-grandson of the common executioner in Kirk's time [Colonel Kirke at the time of the Monmouth Rebellion of 1685], the present finisher of the criminal law in Taunton Deane. Old Otway, it seems, used a singular method in the execution of his victims; they were frequently forced by Kirk's 'lambs' in great numbers, to Pen Elm gallows, where Otway waited with his halters to receive them. Seizing the unfortunate, he first made fast the cord to his neck, and then throwing the other end over the transom beam of the gibbet, instantly caught it and run up his man, uttering at the same time in a grotesque and wanton way, 'Wish !!!', a sound not unlike that used by a great cricketer when he strikes in his most forcible way. Having secured the rope's end, Otway took the next in turn, still making the same sort of sound, in the same wanton manner. From this conduct he acquired the appelation of 'Wish Joshua', so long as he existed; and his descendants, for the office is hereditary, enjoys it at this moment. There is hardly an urchin schoolboy to be found in Taunton, that upon meeting the hangman does not run up to him, imitating with resentful gesticulations the drag of the rope, crying out 'Wish, Joshua'. So accustomed to this is the poor fellow, that he takes it all without reply: and so impressed is everyone with the remembrance of the Taunton tragedy, that not a being could be found to remedy the insult.'

The Otways were only called on to execute two further victims at Stone Gallows. On 10 April 1809 James Taylor, aged 23, was hanged for shooting John Dyer, a coachman, and wounding another man at a Bath inn. The young murderer had been married for only a few months and his behaviour while under sentence was 'truly penitent and exemplary'. In fact the letters he wrote and an account of his imprisonment were later published under the title *Divine Mercy Exemplified* (1813).

The last person to suffer the final penalty of the law at Stone Gallows was 18-year-old Thomas Gage *alias* Tarr on 8 April 1810. The previous November he had taken a hatchet and savagely murdered his mistress, Sarah Styling, a farmer's wife at Goathurst, before robbing her house of a collection of rings. He persistently denied the crime until a few hours before the execution, when he confessed. In the chaplain's opinion, 'a more hardened villain in so early life perhaps was never executed'.

Less than four years after Gage died at the end of his rope, Stone Gallows seems to have disappeared from the local scene. The *Taunton Courier* of 13 January 1814 carried an anonymous letter signed only 'An inhabitant of Bishops Hull'. Referring to the nuisance of the gibbet close to the roadside called the Stone Gallows, the correspondent remarked that it was 'difficult to conceive why an object should be thus preserved which is so painfully uncongenial in the reflections to which it gives rise, with the soothing features of the surrounding scenery'. He urged that, as no execution had taken place there for several years, it should be removed. As all subsequent executions ordered at Taunton Assizes took place at Ilchester, there seems little doubt that it was soon after 1814 that the gallows were finally taken down. Others were indeed hanged at Taunton, but only after the county gaol was moved to the town from Ilchester. A further fourteen men and two women met their end at Wilton Gaol between 1844 and 1884; publicly on the prison roof until 1867.

The final destruction of Stone Gallows seems to be linked with James Billet, the surgeon and occulist who in 1816 founded an eye infirmary in Taunton and later gave his name to Billet Street. He had a house at Rumwell and stones, including the great boulder which gave its name to the gallows, are variously described as being used to build a wall around the lawn or to pave the floor of the hall. Billet also obtained the articulated skeleton of one of the men hanged at Stone Gallows. Some say it was the remains of the last to suffer, Thomas Gage *alias* Tarr. At the Eye Infirmary's last home, at the top of Compass Hill, the skeleton was kept in a long case about the size of a grandfather clock. When the infirmary finally closed in 1904 the skeleton was given to East Reach Hospital to be used for teaching purposes – the final grisly relic of centuries of violent death beside the road to Wellington.

30
COMING OF AGE

TODAY our children reach the age of majority at 18. In my younger days, which once seemed like yesterday and now seem so far away, it was 21. Just supposing birth and baptismal records had never been invented and you were called on to prove that you were of age, how would you do it ? You might call on older relatives and friends to testify to your date of birth, and they in turn might relate it to earth-shattering or parochial events like the year of the Great Train Robbery, Kennedy's assassination, the decimalisation of the currency or the introduction of traffic wardens.

In the Middle Ages, when the inheritance of those under-age was enjoyed by their overlords, it was vital to be able to fix the date of your birth so that you could enter into your lands and possessions. A hearing to establish this and the document that recorded it were known as a Proof of Age and the earliest that we possess for Somerset was for John son and heir of Ralph Huscarl. It was taken at Somerton on Monday the morrow of St Laurence in the 15th year of King Edward I – to you and me, 11 August 1287.

William de Godmanston recalled that young John was born at Eastrip near Bruton on the Ash Wednesday following the Battle of Evesham, 10 February 1266, and remembered being present at his baptism by Canon John de Aure in St Mary's, Bruton. William de Gratelegh witnessed the purification of Hawise, John's mother, after the birth and Nicholas le Mareschal heard about it from his neighbour, Alice, John's godmother.

Already it should begin to be clear how these unique documents conjure up medieval life in freeze-frame fashion. Andrew son of Nicholas Braunche was born at Frome on 29 December 1311. George Michel attended his christening at Frome parish church and was present when a note of the birth was inscribed in the chronicle of Longleat Priory by one of the canons, John Thurstan. John Waspray fixed it in his mind because his daughter was married on the very next day. The birth was announced to the happy father by John Wilichet while Richard de Carswelshaie, clearly an old retainer, was serving at the table. At nearby Buckland

Dinham John de Dynham was holding a feast after his wife had been purified following the birth of her first-born daughter. Into the room burst Robert Redespray to announce little Andrew's birth, as five of the guests testified over 20 years later.

William son and heir of William de la Planke was born at Curry Mallet on 2 October 1325. Sir Henry de Lorty and three other knights remembered that they were hunting in Curry Mallet park where their dogs seized a fat barren doe. On their way back they met the christening party coming away from the church. Three other witnesses had concluded a deal that day with the lord of Curry Mallet, Nicholas de Poyntz, to pay £220 for timber, or 'great wood' as they termed it. Walter de Romesy was born that same year. John le Doo, who was at the christening at Chilthorne Domer, was wounded by robbers on his way home to Coker. Walter's father, John de Romesey, could not hand round cigars but gave a bow and three arrows to John Turk to commemorate the occasion. William de Cheyne fixed the date of his son Edmund's birth at Clevedon even more generously by handing out a bow and six barbed arrows with peacocks' feathers to at least two of the guests at the baptismal service.

When John de Beauchamp was born at Stoke-sub-Hamdon in 1330 John Huchouns came with a message from the abbot of Athelney to the father while he was at the baby's christening in the free chapel of St Nicholas, Huchouns receiving the gift of a robe for his pains. Presents were well to the fore in fixing the birth of Joan daughter of Thomas Chastelayne at Dinnington in 1348. John Vincent, one of the godfathers, went home with two cartloads of wood, John Leddred pocketed a silk purse from the girl's mother after holding the manor court there, and Nicholas Cadebury an axe with a cord when he interrupted the baby's father in making a plan for his new hall. On the day of the christening the father went sporting in Donyatt park with John Bruyn, where they killed a doe with their bows and arrows. Bruyn finished the day with the doe skin as a final baptismal present.

At the time Thomas son and heir of Gilbert de Edyngdon was baptised in the free chapel at Edington on the Polden Hills in 1341, five witnesses came round to help him lift the timber for building a chamber. Gilbert gave them each supper and a buckskin to remember the date. On the same day and in the same chapel John Knygh and four others agreed jointly to buy a grange at Shapwick from the abbot of Glastonbury and the date of their bond established the date of the christening. The Saturday after the birth Gilbert was hunting with Robert Purveour on 'a downe called Cantok by Edyngton', the Quantock Hills, and presented

Robert with a white greyhound to mark the event.

There are other Proofs of Age for Somerset but not many. They demonstrate that the highspots in the lives of the medieval gentry were clearly feasting, hunting and building, probably in that order. However brief the account, for a moment we are there: as in 1344 when Sir Richard Lovel threw a great banquet at Marsh near Wincanton to entertain men like Henry Peytevyn or John de Lotesham; men who would be summoned over 20 years later to testify to the birth of his great-grandson, young Richard Chambernoun.

The cottage at Winsford in which Ernest Bevin first saw the light of day on 7 March 1881.

31

BEVIN AND THE BUTCHER

IT has always been accepted that the great socialist, Ernest Bevin, never knew the identity of his own father. His birth on 7 March 1881 to Diana Bevin, a 40-year-old widow, in the little Exmoor village of Winsford has often been contrasted with the major political success that he was later to achieve. Every reference book and biography, however, is agreed that the name of his natural father is now unlikely to be discovered. Even Lord Bullock in his great two-volume work on Bevin confessed in 1960 'who his father was remains unknown'.

Bevin's mother, Diana, born at Winsford in 1841, was the second child and eldest daughter of a labourer, Thomas Tudball, and his wife, Mary Volter. In 1864 Diana married the Winsford sexton's son, 34-year-old farm labourer, William Bevin, and by him produced a daughter and son, both born at Winsford. The family then moved to Howetown in the adjacent parish of Exton where a further two sons were born. It has always been known that Ernest, Diana's youngest child, was illegitimate but it has never been acknowledged that two earlier sons, Albert and Frederick, were also born out of wedlock, in 1875 and 1877, as clearly stated in the Winsford parish register.

The accepted version of events is that William Bevin took his family across the Bristol Channel to Wales in search of work and that Diana later returned to Winsford without him, describing herself as a widow. There is certainly a gap of four years, 1871-75, in the births of her seven children, although judging from the annual payments of Joyce's charity money she was in Winsford with her husband at Easter 1872 and back alone in the parish by Easter 1873.

The key document, not available for public consultation at the time all the major works on Bevin were researched and written, is the 1881 Census taken on 3 April of that year, immediately after Ernest's birth. This shows Diana as a laundress with her four youngest sons, including one-month-old Ernest, living as a lodger with William Pearce (his name was usually spelt 'Pearse').

Thus enter Pearse as candidate for Ernest Bevin's natural father. Born in 1816 at Selworthy near Minehead on the West Somerset coast, he was the second son of another William Pearse. Farming first at Blackford and then at Allerford, both in Selworthy, the father brought his family to Winsford in the 1820s, where he died in 1857. In his will he left £10 a year to his son William and ordered his executors to finish for William the newly-erected cottage at Winsford which was to become Ernest Bevin's birthplace. The eldest son John followed his father into agriculture at Winsford Farm but William and a younger son, Richard, both became butchers.

A few years before his father's death William married Leah, a girl from Tiverton in Devon, and established himself at nearby Dulverton, where a son, William, was born in 1856. He then returned to Winsford to the cottage left to him by his father, and there a second child, Emma, arrived in 1859. Leah and her two children had left William by 1881, probably some years before. She was 18 years younger than her husband and he had clearly not made a success of butchering, never rating even a mention in the trade directories of the time. In 1872 he was fined for refusing to pay his rates and towards the end of his life he was reduced to receiving charity payments and the parish's winter dole of peas and bacon.

All contemporary accounts agree that Diana was a good and loving mother and she was clearly not the sort of person to enter lightly into a succession of relationships which would have resulted in three illegitimate children by different fathers. She applied for no paternity orders at Dulverton Petty Sessions and was never taken into Dulverton Union Workhouse. The evidence suggests strongly that these children were the product of a single stable relationship and that the father was the man with whom Diana was living at the time that Ernest Bevin was born. If Diana was indeed a widow, as she claimed, it is likely that her alliance would have been with a man such as William Pearse, deserted by his wife and unable to marry her.

For whatever reason, the union eventually turned sour. Perhaps the moral feelings of their neighbours made it impossible for William and Diana to continue living under the same roof. He was over 20 years older than her and she may have fallen out of love with him as his wife Leah had done before. Soon after Ernest was born Diana left Pearse's home and moved to a cottage on the outskirts of the village. According to Bullock she took work as a home help, served as midwife and assisted in the kitchen of the thatched Royal Oak Inn which still ministers to Winsford drinkers in the centre of the village.

After 1884 she drew no charity from the parish, although fined 2s, with several others, for failing to send her children to school. Worn out by a life which must have been both harsh and hard, she died in 1889 aged only 48. Eight-year-old Ernest shook the dust of Winsford off his feet and went to Devon to live with his half-sister Mary and her husband.

Short of blood tests, the identity of the natural father of an illegitimate child is impossible to prove absolutely. At this distance of time Ernest Bevin's parentage is as certain as it is possible to be, given the nature of the evidence.

William Pearse survived Diana by only two years, dying in May 1891 aged 74. No grave stones mark their final resting places in the little churchyard at Winsford. Only the plaque which singles out Ernest Bevin's birthplace testifies to a love affair which gave this country one of its most prominent statesmen.

Winsford parish church where Diana Bevin and Thomas Pearse were buried.

32

HIGH TREASON

WHEN I first arrived in Somerset in 1967, it soon became evident to me that the prevailing opinion was that nothing of note had ever happened in the county apart from the Monmouth Rebellion of 1685. Certainly no other incident had had such a profound impact on the folk consciousness and folk memory of the county, as was witnessed by the many stories which had grown up around that event. An isolated house was pointed out as where Judge Jeffreys had held his Bloody Assizes; an isolated tree as one from which the rebels had been hanged.

The luckless James, Duke of Monmouth: defeated at Sedgemoor and executed on Tower Hill.

Judge Jeffreys is claimed to have held 'summary courts' here at the George Inn, Norton St Philip, but there is no evidence whatsoever for this. The inn building dates from the later 14th century: a miraculous medieval survival. Samuel Pepys is believed to have dined here in 1668 and the house reputedly provided a shelter for the Duke of Monmouth on his retreat from Bristol and Bath in June 1685.

Such tales are important not because they are reliable in historical terms, which often they are not, but because they show how large the rebellion and its brutal aftermath bulked in the popular mind. The danger is that so many of them have been reported as totally factual, particularly in recent years.

Thus Shirley Toulson in *The Mendip Hills* (1984) writes of Judge Jeffreys holding 'his summary courts' at the George Inn, Norton St Philip, and 'an emergency court' at Axbridge, where Jacob Tripp was condemned. We know that Jeffreys held his Somerset Assizes only in Taunton and Wells and at no other venue within the county whatsoever. There were indeed executions at both Norton and Axbridge but those who suffered were tried and convicted at Wells. Tripp was sentenced to be hanged at Axbridge but, 'being unconscious and dying of gaol fever', was cold-bloodedly executed in Wells Market Place. These fictitious trials are also reiterated as fact by the Rev Alan Holt in *Old North Somerset* (1987), who adds a further one at Langridge Court, although expressing a justified scepticism about the last.

A local tradition speaks of another trial at Cathanger, a Domesday manor and fine mansion in Fivehead, adding the corroborative detail of a secret passage from the house to Curry Mallet Manor, supposedly dug

Judge George Jeffreys: the scourge of the West in 1685.

by the rebels fleeing from Jeffreys' justice – over a mile as the mole burrows. Inevitably the tunnel has defied all attempts to locate it. The story of the trial was clearly inspired by the hanging connotation of the house's name (which in fact means 'the slope where wild cats live', occurring as 'Cathangre' in the Domesday Book of 1086) and the fact that the present building was built by a judge, albeit a 16th century one – John Walsh. Needless to say, none of the rebels are known to have perished at Fivehead.

There are also unfounded stories concerned with execution sites. The name of the Hanging Chapel, which spans the road across the Hill at Langport, clearly suggested to the popular mind that the arched building was where the three rebels who met their deaths in the town were dispatched. It is thus identified even in the otherwise excellent *The Monmouth Rebellion* by W. MacDonald Wigfield (1980). There is no contemporary evidence for it as the execution site, and the chapel itself was referred to as the 'Hawninge Chapel' as early as 1575, over a century before the rebellion.

Another notable arch long associated with the Monmouth Rising is the gateway leading to the manor-house at Cothelstone on the Quan-

The Hanging Chapel at Langport – unlikely site of a triple execution.

tocks. Col Richard Bovet and Thomas Blackmore are stated in a host of books on Somerset to have been hanged from the archway. There is no doubt that the two men were indeed executed in Cothelstone parish but the gradual process by which the arch was identified as their gallows is an intriguing one. John Oldmixon's *History of England during the Reigns of the Royal House of Stuart* (1730) is the earliest work that I have managed to trace which supplies the background to the executions.

'Lord Ralph Stawel', wrote Oldmixon (exhibiting a profound weakness for capital letters to add force to his arguments), 'tho' a staunch Abhorrer, was so shock'd at the Report of his [Judge Jeffrey's] Cruelty and Brutality that he would not see him, tho' then in the Zenith of his Grandeur; and Jefferies in Resentment, ordered Col Bovet of Taunton to be hang'd at Cotholstone, a Parish which belong'd to Lord Stawel, contrary to that Lord's good Liking, tho' Bovet had been one of the Sequestrators of that and other Estates of the Stawels'.

No reference here to the execution site and Oldmixon's account was repeated, without embellishment, in Richard Locke's *The Western Rebellion* (1782): Locke in turn being cited in Joshua Toulmin's *History of Taunton* (1791) and James Savage's revision of Toulmin's work in 1822. George Roberts in his *Life of James, Duke of Monmouth* (1844) added the detail that Bovet was to be executed 'close to' Stawell's house, while Lord Macauley's *History of England* (1866) elaborated the story by stating that Stawell 'was punished by having a corpse suspended in chains at his park gate', quoting only Locke as his source. An 18th century map of Cothelstone manor shows the park gate situated high up on the Quantock ridge, although it is doubtful whether Macauley would have known this. The first author that I can find who identifies the manor archway with the hangings was J.Ll.P. Creswell in his *Land of Quantock* (1903), over two centuries after the event: hardly contemporary evidence for the fact.

It was almost inevitable that Taunton, as the focus of the initial rising, should in turn attract its Monmouth myths. The garden behind the old Green Dragon Inn in High Street, now an estate agency, was identified in a recent local paper as the location of several impromptu executions. Again there is only authority for 19 such deaths at the hands of Col Kirke, without trial, soon after the battle and a further 19 following the Assizes: in both cases in the Market Place, now the Parade.

One of the most persistent Taunton stories, recorded from the earlier 19th century, concerns the Tudor Tavern, now a restaurant, in Fore Street. According to this tale, the property was the town house of Sir William Portman, the man entrusted with escorting the captured Duke of Monmouth to London. The 14th century house certainly belonged to the Portmans but was only one of many that they held in the town. The family leased it to a succession of tenants, one of whom, cloth merchant Thomas Trowbridge, added the picturesque half-timbered facade in 1578. In a 1642 lease to Aldred Seaman, husband of Trowbridge's granddaughter, Sir William Portman reserved to himself and his servants the use of the Great Chamber at the front of the house during the Assizes and Sessions in the town. Later leases, now lost, apparently specified such a use at the time of Parliamentary elections. From these reservations may have sprung the story that Judge Jeffreys himself was accommodated there during the three days of the Bloody Assizes at Taunton.

In 1685 the building was occupied under the Portmans by Thomas Baker, a 42-year-old grocer, and a prominent nonconformist in the town, a trustee of Paul's Meeting and one of the original Conservators of the River Tone, charged with improving and maintaining the navigation up the river from Bridgwater. Two of his daughters, Mary and Elizabeth, had been among those schoolgirls, the celebrated Maids of Taunton, who had presented banners to Monmouth on his arrival in the town. Baker himself was described by the Duke of Albemarle as 'one of Monmouth Privy Council, very rich'. A month after the Bloody Assizes a warrant was issued for his arrest for treasonable practices, but he was later pardoned and nominated as mayor of Taunton under a new borough charter of 1688 which never took effect. Indeed, if one had to choose the least likely Tauntonian in whose house Judge Jeffreys might have spent his nights in the town, Thomas Baker would probably be the leading contender. In all likelihood Jeffreys probably lodged at Taunton Castle, as did those judges who were to try cases at later Assizes held in the town.

Myths and legends form a vital and revealing part of our heritage but they should never be recounted as history, blinding us to the way things really happened.

33
GOLDEN GAULDEN

EIGHT miles northwest of Taunton in the little parish of Tolland lies the small but attractive manor-house of Gaulden, impeccably restored since 1966 with a new garden imaginatively created by its present owners, Mr and Mrs James le Gendre Starkie. The accepted accounts of its long history, however, leave much to be desired.

In 1979 there appeared a book entitled *The Country House Guide*, supplying full details of privately-owned properties throughout the country and intended as a companion volume to *The National Trust Guide*. The description of Gaulden Manor includes the following remarks on its history:

'Gaulden was apparently a sub-manor of Tolland, and in the 12th century it belonged to Taunton Priory. During the 1560s it was leased to James Turberville, former Bishop of Exeter, who had been imprisoned for some years in the Tower of London for refusing to take the Oath of Supremacy. Between 1618 and 1630 Gaulden was owned by Christopher Wolcott, whose family then migrated to America, but the Turbervilles returned in 1639 – and remained here for a hundred years.'

Almost every 'fact' in this paragraph can be challenged. Gaulden was not a sub-manor but a manor which originated from three gifts of land in Tolland by Andrew de Bovedon to Taunton Priory at an unspecified date but probably in the mid 13th century. It certainly had a manor court by 1319 and tenants holding by copyhold tenure at that date.

The manor was retained by Taunton Priory until its dissolution at the hands of Henry VIII in 1539. Gaulden was then held by the Crown until 1545 when it was sold to William Standish. Thence it passed to Francis Southwell and his wife in 1551, by whom it was granted in 1565 to George Mynne, who died in 1581. Mynne's widow, Elizabeth, her second husband, Nicholas Boteler, and Mynne's son, Robert, succeeded and held the manor-until Robert sold it in 1615 to John Turberville of Sampford Peverel in Devon. Turberville evidently bought the premises for his son, also John, who married in 1639, rebuilt Gaulden manor house with its intriguing plasterwork in or around 1642 and died in 1677.

Gaulden Manor: the home of the Sellicks, the Turbervilles and the Starkies – but definitely not the Wolcotts !

The Turbervilles owned Gaulden until 1699 when the second John's daughter-in-law and grandson sold it to Edward Galhampton.

The story of Bishop John Turberville spending his declining years at Gaulden originated with a paper written about a century ago which misdated the plasterwork in the hall at Gaulden to the 16th century and drew erroneous conclusions from its biblical subjects and the Turberville coat of arms. There is reason to believe that Bishop Turberville died in the Tower of London and was never released to live out his retirement at Gaulden or, indeed, anywhere else. Recent publicity for the manor-house has made great play of supposed links with the Turbervilles of Bere Regis in Dorset, immortalised by Thomas Hardy in his novel, *Tess of the Durbervilles*. The John Turberville who moved into Gaulden manor house in 1642 was indeed ultimately descended from the Dorset family, but his father, grandfather, great-grandfather and great-great-grandfather all lived in Devon. Their own links with Bishop Turberville were remote, John being fourth cousin three times removed with a common ancestor as far back as Sir Robert Turberville of Bere Regis, who died in 1424.

None of the lords of Gaulden manor lived in the manor-house until John Turberville moved into the building in 1642: so who did ? A family called Sellick or Selake received the grant of a lease of the manor house in 1525 and may have occupied it even before that date. They were certainly living there in 1560 and 1615 and a pedigree registered with the College of Arms in 1672 indicates that the family continued there until they removed to Nether Stowey, where their most prominent member, the Ven John Sellick, Archdeacon of Bath 1661-90, was raised. The Sellicks were living at Gaulden manor-house throughout the time that Bishop Turberville and Christopher Wolcott were supposed to have occupied it.

We have seen how the story of Bishop John Turberville at Gaulden originated. The Wolcott story started in a different way. In 1630 Henry Wolcott of Tolland became one of the early emigrants to America. There he founded a new dynasty which over the years became one of the leading families in the State of Connecticut. Indeed, today there is not only a town but also a county named Tolland in that State.

In 1639 Henry Wolcott inherited the Tolland lands on the death of his brother Christopher and with them certain documents: in particular a grant made in 1618 by the lord of Gaulden manor, Robert Mynne, to Christopher Wolcott. The lands in question were loosely described as messuages, lands, meadows, pastures, mills, tenements and heredita- ments then held in Tolland and Lydeard St Lawrence by Christopher Wolcott (and his father and grandfather before him), and in Tolland by William Pyke. Both holdings were described as being held by copy of court roll. As we know that the manor-house and its lands were leasehold by 1409 and thus not copyhold, we also know that the Wol- cotts could not have held the manor-house under this deed.

In 1881 Samuel Wolcott privately published in New York a weighty tome entitled *Memorial of Henry Wolcott, one of the first settlers of Windsor, Connecticut, and of some of his descendants.* To Mr Wolcott a grant of land in the manor of Gaulden unquestionably meant a grant of the manor- house, and ever since that date generations of Wolcott descendants have made individual and collective pilgrimages to what they have regarded as the family ancestral home. It is, however, abundantly clear from family correspondence and other Tolland documents that the property held first by Christopher Wolcott and then by Henry was not Gaulden manor- house at all, but Tolland Mill.

In England Henry Wolcott was described at various dates either as a husbandman or a clothier. His family were of yeomen stock. Their signa- tures to deeds and leases show that they were certainly literate although their seals usually bore only their personal monograms. As soon as it was believed that the family had owned a manor-house, however, the idea originated, either with English researchers or American descendants, that the family must have been of the landed gentry and must, therefore, have had a coat of arms. The fact that the family appeared in none of the Heralds' Visitations of Somerset seems not to have concerned them. American descendants, unable to find any arms for a family named Wolcott, calmly appropriated the arms and subsequently the ancestry of the family of Walcot of Walcot in Lydbury, Shropshire. These arms bore three chess rooks and the Wolcotts even went so far as to take as their own the Shropshire Walcots' tradition that their ancestor was granted the coat after checkmating Henry V at chess with a rook. The net result is that, thanks to the gifts of well-meaning Americans, the west window of Tolland Church bears a representation in stained glass of the Shropshire family's coat of arms, to which they have no claim whatsoever, and a similar gift adorns the manor-house itself. Ironically, recent research has shown that Henry Wolcott's wife, Elizabeth Saunders, had a maternal aunt, Elizabeth Blake, who married Robert Sellick of Gaulden. Thus, although Henry Wolcott never appears to have lived at Gaulden manor-house, through his wife he had an uncle and aunt who did!

Let me not go too far. The hold of Bishop Turberville and the Wolcotts may have been laboriously prised loose from Gaulden manor-house, but the building still possesses a long and interesting history and, may I say, is well worth a visit.

The coat of arms of the Walcots of Shropshire, appropriated by the American Wolcott family.

34
WHAT'S IN A NAME?

A N archivist's day-to-day work, like that of any other job, inevitably has its boring elements: its routine. For instance, tracing the owner-ship of a house through the centuries means searching through seem-ingly interminable lists of names in sources such as rate books and Land Tax assessments. To brighten up the day one tends to keep an eye open for unusual or intriguing names and one of my former colleagues, Celia Parker, started to make a systematic collection of these. Since she left Somerset for the delights of Sheffield I have continued this pursuit and find it amazing how otherwise sensible parents can saddle their offspring with ridiculous names.

In the days when a classical education at one of the old endowed grammar schools was what separated the upper classes from the workers, some families seem to have been determined to display their learning. Thus Erasmus Phrase was married at St Decuman's in 1685, Narcissus Moorshead Pinch was christened at Walcot, Bath, in 1801, and Lucius Junius Brutus Tapp passed away at Kilmersdon in 1840. An illegitimate child born at Stoke St Michael in 1803, as though to belie his origins, was christened Fortunatus Woborn. A spurious gentility or an attempt to brighten up a run-of-the-mill surname presumably led to the naming of Parthenia Higgins, married at Merriott in 1787, and of Pollidore Mosse at Beckington in 1697. One example which fell on stony ground during one of my lectures in the Mendip area was that of a 19th century Somerset clergyman called the Rev Cicero Rabbits. I had not anticipated that the surname was still relatively common and there was more than one bearing it in my audience.

A note of romance was occasionally introduced in the naming of girls. Astrea Oceana Egerton occurs at Milverton in 1827, Balmarina Barley at Wells in 1795, and Czarina Vinnel at Frome in 1781. My favourite in this category, however, has to be Arabia Herring of Pitminster in 1744.

The idea that certain virtues could be instilled in children through their names presumably led to the christening of Manley Power at Walcot in 1782 and of Repentance Button at Frome in the same year.

Friendly Churches occurred at Meare in 1864 and Gracious Fathers died at Henstridge in 1842.

The reverse was clearly the case in the naming of bastard child Misfortune Pope at Baltonsborough in 1720 and Freelove Nash at Tellisford in 1752. A most unfortunate case was that of the woman prosecuted at Nether Stowey in 1621 for leading an immoral life – Temptation Brewer.

Major national events or heroes inevitably took their toll. At the height of the South African War children in Taunton were given the Christian names Pretoria, Bloemfontein, Mafeking, Ladysmith and Baden-Powell. Three years after one great naval battle, Trafalgar Nelson Francis was christened at Walcot in 1808 and Napoleon Trotman was clearly named by a Francophile at Frome in 1825. When Parliamentary reform was in the air in 1831 Harriet Reform French was baptised at Taunton St Mary's. The choicest was surely a boy who first saw the light of day at Widcombe, Bath, in 1916. The minister noted in the register that the lad's father was serving in Egypt before proceeding to name him Fendland Montague Pyramid Haynes.

To modern ears some names were just downright silly. Elias Ferret was married in 1817 and I found Sweet Marjorum in 1709, both at Bath. Tory Churchouse cropped up at Meare in 1846, Overlong Cottle in 1813 at Chard, and in 1815 at Frome – Otto Rotten.

There is one 18th century marriage at Yatton, however, that shines forth above all others as having been clearly made in heaven, although at the time its significance probably went wholly unappreciated. It was on 12 July 1762 between Samuel Sage and – Hannah Onion !

The delightful union of Sage and Onion at Yatton in 1762.

ACKNOWLEDGEMENTS

I am grateful to the following owners of documents deposited at the Somerset Record Office for permission to reproduce their archives as illustrations.

Col Walter F. Luttrell, Mr William A. Sanford, Mr Seymour Blake, Mr John Wolseley, the late Mr William B. Clatworthy, and the ministers of individual parishes: the Rev Dudley Ractliffe (Dowlish Wake), Rev Trevor Farmiloe (Hemington), Rev Dan Richards (Ilchester), Rev David Osmond (Pendomer), Canon Ronald Tostevin (Somerton), Rev Roger Spurr (Stogumber), Preb Dick Acworth (Taunton St Mary Magdalene), Rev Charles Hadley (Ubley), Rev Richard Russell (Widcombe, Bath), and Rev John Ruffle (Yatton).

Principal Sources

Abbreviations

S.R.O. – archive sources in Somerset Record Office, Taunton
S.R.S. – volumes published by the Somerset Record Society
PSANHS – *Proceedings of the Somerset Archaeological & Natural History Society*

1. The Rector Vanishes

Western Gazette, 17 Jan – 28 Feb 1868; 4 Mar 1881
Victoria History of Somerset, iv, 151-5
Burke's Landed Gentry (1952) s.v. Speke
Burke's Peerage (1938) s.v. Fuller
Devon & Cornwall Notes and Queries, xxi, 151-7

2. The Viking *Weston Mercury*, Dec 1985

PSANHS, xxi, 1-27
Gover, Mawer & Stenton, *Place Names of Devon*, i (1931), 62-3
S.R.S. v, 50
S.R.O., Q/RLa 24
British Library, Egerton MS 3034
Stenton, Sir Frank, *Anglo-Saxon England* (3rd edn. 1971), 243, 245-6
Collinson, Rev John, *History of Somerset* (1791), i, 202
Anglo-Saxon Chronicle, anno 878
Lawrence, Berta, *Somerset Legends* (1973), 79-83
Greswell, W.H.P., *Dumnonia and the Valley of the Parret* (1922), 185

3. Unnatural Death

Somerset & Dorset Notes & Queries, xxxi, 451-72
S.R.O., DD/L, P31/1

4. Whiggish Christenings

S.R.O., Ilchester parish registers
Victoria History of Somerset, iii, 196
Western Flying Post, 22 June 1818

5. Eureka !

S.R.O., DD/SB 31/7
S.R.O., DD/CT 77
S.R.O., DD/SF 3066
Sunday Telegraph, April 1986

6. The Highwayman and the Grazier
Western Flying Post, 1 Nov 1830; 11, 18, 25 Apr 1831
S.R.O., Q/AGi 15/3
Somerset & Dorset Notes & Queries, xxviii, 169

7. Enmore Effigies
Photocopies of letter and wills provided by Miss E.M. Porter of Mayfield, Sussex, through Mrs Audrey Mead
Haining, Peter, *The Man who was Frankenstein* (1979)
Dictionary of National Biography, s.v. Andrew Crosse

8. Audacious Avalon
Finberg, H.P.R., *West-Country Historical Studies* (1969)
Finberg, H.P.R., *Lucerna* (1964)
Carley, J.P., *Glastonbury Abbey* (1988)
William of Malmesbury, *The Early History of Glastonbury Abbey*, ed. John Scott (1981)
John of Glastonbury, *The Chronicle of Glastonbury Abbey*, ed. J.P. Carley (1985)
Treharne, R.F., *The Glastonbury Legends* (1967)
Deanesly, Margaret, *The Pre-Conquest Church in England* (2nd edn. 1963)
Maltwood, Katherine, *A Guide to Glastonbury's Temple of the Stars* (1935)
Maltwood, Katherine, *Air View Supplement to a Guide to Glastonbury's Temple of the Stars* (1937)
Burrow, Ian, 'Star-spangled Avalon' in *Popular Archaeology*, Feb 1983

9. Manchester Jack
Census Returns, Taunton, 1851, 1861
S.R.O., parish registers, St Mary Magdalene, Holy Trinity, Taunton; Misterton
S.R.O., rate books, St Mary Magdalene, Taunton; Bishops Hull
Taunton Courier, 15 July 1829; 1 Mar 1865
Somerset County Herald Notes & Queries (1904), 324-5, 345
Goldsworthy, E.F., *Reminiscences of Taunton* (1975), 7

10. The Incestuous Baronet
S.R.O., DD/GL 187
Western Flying Post, 15 Jan 1765
History of Parliament, the Commons, 1754-90, ed. L. Namier & J. Brooke (1964), s.v. Pynsent
The Complete Baronetage, ed. G.E.C., iv, 145-6
Burke's Extinct and Dormant Baronetage
Mounter, Arthur, *A Social History of Curry Rivel in the 19th Century* (priv. print.)

11. One Woman's Legs
Baring-Gould, Sabine, *Devonshire Characters and Strange Events* (1908), 177-80

12. The Heavenly Cannonball
S.R.O., parish registers of Stogumber and Monksilver
Devon Record Office, parish registers of St Budeaux, Plymouth
Collections of Thomas Hearne (Oxfordshire Historical Soc xliii), 120
Jennings, James, *Poems* (1810)
Victoria History of Somerset, v, 181
Sydenham, G.F., *History of the Sydenham Family*, ed. A.T. Cameron (1928), 517-25
Somerset & Dorset Notes & Queries, xxv, 200; xxxii, 599
Vivian, J.L., *Visitations of Devon* (1895), 247, 299

13. Drink Up Thee Zyder !
Files of the *Western Flying Post*, 1763-67
S.R.O., DD/DR 69/8

14. Dragon or Wyvern?

Somerset Year Book, 1922, 98-99
Oxford Companion to the Decorative Arts, 301
Somerset Folklore, ed. R.L. Tongue & K.M. Briggs (1965), 129-31
Speculum, viii, 223-35
Somerset & Dorset Notes & Queries, xxii, 244-49

15. A Royal By-Blow?

The Times, 8 Sept 1915
South Wales Daily Post, 8 Sept 1915
West Somerset Free Press, 9 Oct 1960; 3 Sept 1982
Census Returns, 1871-91, Withypool and Exford
S.R.O., DD/IR, T 13/4
Kelly's Directories of Somerset
Information supplied by Mr W.J.H. Thomas and Mr Alan Steer

16. Unbroken Links

Victoria History of Somerset, v (1985): articles on Crowcombe, Nettlecombe and East Quantoxhead by R.J.E. Bush, R.W. Dunning and M.C. Siraut
Bush, R.J.E., 'Nettlecombe Court', in *Field Studies*, iii (1970), 275-86
Dodd, Dudley, *Dunster Castle* (National Trust guide book)

17. The Clerk of the Weather

S.R.O., parish registers of Pendomer and Ubley

18. Cudgel Playing

Oxford English Dictionary
Wright's Dialect Dictionary
Elworthy, F.T., *West Somerset Word Book* (1888)
Hole, Christine, *English Sports and Pastimes* (1949)
Oxford Companion to Sports and Games
Wedmore Chronicle
Somerset & Dorset Notes & Queries, iii, 305
Parson Woodforde's Diary
Taunton Courier, various entries
Western Flying Post, various 18th century entries
Somerset County Herald, 28 May 1921; 30 May 1964

19. The Burning of Women

Western Flying Post, 10 Sept 1753; 13 May 1765
S.R.O., Durleigh parish register
History of Parliament, the Commons, 1790-1820, ed. R.G. Thorne, iv (1986), 141-2

20. A Right Royal Day

British Library, Add MS 30,277, f.34
Bush, Robin, *The Book of Taunton* (1977) 75-81, 101
Chandler, David, *Sedgemoor 1685* (1985), 90
Taunton Courier, 20 Aug 1856
Patton, Thomas, *Wise Men of the West* (1916)

21. The Vigorous Vigors

S.R.O., Hemington parish registers
S.R.S., lxiii, 454
John of Glastonbury, *The Chronicle of Glastonbury Abbey*, ed. J.P. Carley (1985), 207-8
Farmer, D.H., *Oxford Dictionary of Saints* (1978), 391

22. V.C.H. Som.

Victoria History of Somerset, vols. iii-v

23. Monksilver and Monksilver

Title deeds of 2 Kilkenny Villas, held by the Abbey National Building Society !
Census Returns, 1881, Monksilver
S.R.O., Monksilver parish registers
Obituaries in *Somerset County Gazette*
DD/CCH 3/4: Marwood Notley's executors' papers

24. Little Jack Horner

Cleverdon, Rev F.W., *History of Mells*, 39
PSANHS, xxx (1884), 58-60
Letters and Papers of Henry VIII, xvii(i), p.533
Opie, I. & P., *Oxford Dictionary of Nursery Rhymes* (1951), 234-7

25. Simply Ripping !

Files of *Somerset County Gazette*, *Western Gazette* and *Pulman's Weekly News*, July –
Sept 1911
Maber, Roy, *Martock Memories* (1977), 49-51

26. The Sea-Faring Bigamist

S.R.O., Q/SR, Epiphany 1842
S.R.O., Somerton parish registers
Taunton Courier, 12 Jan 1842; 16 Aug 1843
Census Returns, 1841-51, Somerton and East Chinnock
S.R.O., Q/AGw 15/5 (gaol description book)
Fairbairn's Crests, s.v. Barnard
The Complete Peerage, s.v. Bakeham

27. The Mistletoe Bough

Marriage Allegation Bonds, ed. A.J. Jewers (1909), 209
Somerset Incumbents, ed. F.W. Weaver (1889), 21

28. The Miller's Tale

S.R.O., parish registers of Taunton St James, Stogursey, Stogumber and Spaxton
S.R.O., DD/TB, wife contract, 1761
Greenwood Tree, x, 48, 142 (from the researches of Mr L.G. Mead)

29. Stone Gallows

Rotuli Hundredorum (Rec. Com.), ii, 125
Somerset County Herald Notes & Queries (1897), 61-2, 325; (1898), 449; (1903), 284-5;
(1905), 148-50; (1907), 28-9
Toulmin, Joshua, *History of Taunton* (1791) – map
25 in. Ordnance Survey maps
S.R.O., DD/SP 23/37
Green, Emanuel, *Bibliotheca Somersetensis*, iii (1902), 348
S.R.O., DD/SAS, BA 9/7; C/2401/10
Humphreys, Arthur, *Fragments of Local History* (1892)
Bush, Robin, *Book of Taunton* (1977), 29, 78, 117
St James's Evening Post, 6-9 May 1738
Sherborne, Dorchester and Taunton Journal, 6 Aug 1829
Western Flying Post, 21 Apr 1741; 3 Apr 1758; 3 Apr 1769; 2 May 1770; 14 Apr
1783; 7, 14 Apr 1788; 20 July, 24 Aug 1789; 9 Apr 1792; 8 Apr 1793; 7 Apr 1794; 9
Apr 1798; 20 Apr 1801
Journal of Capt W. Le Geyt, cited in L.E.J. Brooke's Taunton history notes, Local
History Library, Taunton Castle

30. Coming of Age
Calendars of Inquisitions Post Mortem, vols. ii-xii

31. Bevin and the Butcher
Bullock, Alan, *Life and Times of Ernest Bevin*, i (1960)
Stephens, Mark, *Ernest Bevin* (1981)
S.R.O., parish registers of Winsford, Exton and Selworthy
Winsford parish church, later parish registers
S.R.O., D/P/wins 17/3/77-153
Census returns, 1851-81, Winsford and Exton
S.R.O., DD/ED 273/324 (Pearse)
Kelly's Directories of Somerset
S.R.O., D/PS/dul 1/1-2

32. High Treason
Bush, R.J.E., 'Tudor Tavern, Taunton' in *PSANHS*, cxix, 15-21
Public Record Office, C 66/1125/3

33. Golden Gaulden
The Country House Guide, ed. R. Fedden & J. Kenworthy-Brown (1979)
Hoskins, W.G., & H.P.R. Finberg, *Devonshire Studies* (1952), 367n
S.R.O., Tolland Bishop's Transcripts
S.R.O., DD/SF 3126, 3138
S.R.O., DD/DP, box 33/8; box 34
S.R.O., DD/CH 79
S.R.O., DD/SP 408
S.R.O., D/D/Cd 39
S.R.O., DD/SAS, HV 66/1, p.50
Calendar of Patent Rolls, 1563-66, 270; 1566-69, 43; 1572-75, 255
Calendar of Charter Rolls, 1327-41, 312-18
Letters & Papers of Henry VIII, xx(i), 56, 122
Hugo, Thomas, *History of Taunton Priory* (1860)
Wolcott, S., *Memorial of Henry Wolcott* (1881)
Public Record Office, S.C. 6/Henry VIII/3137

34. What's in a Name ?
S.R.O., parish and non-parochial registers

INDEX